P9-DNA-067

GRANUAILE

The Life and Times of Grace O'Malley
c.1530·1603

A note to the Reader

Grace O'Malley, and in particular the story of her life as presented in this book, is the subject of a record album, written and composed by Shaun Davey (well known for his previous albums *The Brendan Voyage* and *The Pilgrim*).

It takes the form of a suite of songs for a chamber orchestra, augmented by percussion, harp, guitar, uilleann pipes played by Liam O'Flynn, and features the beautiful and versatile singing of Rita Connolly.

The album, titled *Granuaile,* is available on the Tara label: Record No. 3017 (Tara Records, Anne's Lane, Dublin) and is distributed in the UK by Polygram Records.

·TERRA·MARIQUE·POTENS·

Grace O'Malley's Coat of Arms

GRANUAILE

The Life and Times of Grace O'Malley

c.1530•1603

ANNE CHAMBERS

WOLFHOUND PRESS

Reprinted 1991, 1994
© 1988 Anne Chambers

First published 1979
Paperback edition 1983, 1986
New edition 1988
WOLFHOUND PRESS
68 Mountjoy Square,
Dublin 1.

All rights reserved. No part of this book may be reproduced or utilised in any form or by any means, electronic or mechanical, including photography, filming, recording, video recording, photocopying or by any information storage and retrieval system, or otherwise circulated in any form of binding or cover other than that in which it is published, without prior permission in writing from the publisher.

British Library Cataloguing in Publication Data

Chambers, Anne
  Granuaile: the life and times of Grace
  O'Malley c. 1530-1603. – 2nd ed.
  1. Ireland. O'Malley, Grace, 1530-1600?
  I. Title
  941.505'092'4

ISBN 0-86327-213-4

Made and printed in Great Britain by
The Guernsey Press Co. Ltd., Guernsey, Channel Islands.

Cover illustration shows carved figurehead representing Granuaile on *Asgard II,* a brigantine designed for sail training purposes. By kind permission of Coiste an Asgard / Dept. of Defence. Photograph by Liam Blake. Paperback cover design by Flying Colours (Grapevine). Author photo on back cover by Liam Lyons.

ACKNOWLEDGEMENTS

The staff of the National Library of Ireland for their sustained assistance and courtesy: National Museum of Ireland; Public Record Office, Dublin; Public Record Office, London; Office of Public Works, National Monuments Section; Irish Folklore Commission, U.C.D.; Librarian and staff, Galway County Library; Librarian and staff, Mayo County Library; Sir John Ainsworth, National Library of Ireland; D. F. Begley, Genealogical Office, Dublin Castle; T. P. O'Neill, U.C.G.; Professor E. Rynne, U.C.G.; Nicholas Canny, U.C.G.; Professor J. G. Barry, U.C.C.; Lord Altamont, Westport House; Mr. C. S. Gaisford St. Lawrence, Howth Castle; Liam Lyons, Westport; Tom Kennedy, Leixlip. For their research and secretarial assistance: Margaret Chambers, Eleanor Ward, Martina Farah and Grainne Walshe.

CONTENTS

ILLUSTRATIONS

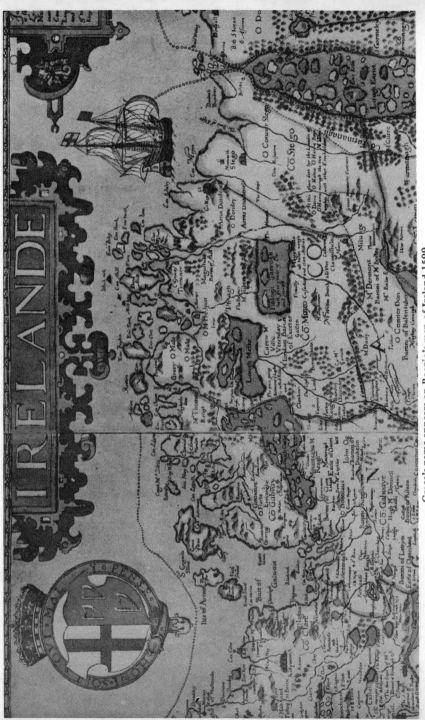

Grace's name appears on Boazio's map of Ireland 1599.

INTRODUCTION

Grace O'Malley or Granuaile is a name associated with
the west of Ireland and more particularly with the western
coastline around Clew Bay. Legends and stories of her
exploits in the sixteenth century abound, some based on
fact exaggerated with the lapse of time, others founded
completely in the realm of fantasy. The name 'Grace
O'Malley' conjures up for some an image of an amazon-
type woman, ruthless and domineering, performing
incredible deeds with no particular end in mind; for others
the name is associated with a figure of fiery patriotism,
whose sole aim in life was to expel the foreign invader
from native soil.

What were the real circumstances surrounding the life
of this remarkable woman? For over 70 years she lived in
one of the more remote regions of Ireland, yet, her name is
recorded for posterity in the Elizabethan State Papers; her
exploits are reported in official state dispatches of such
notables as Sir Henry Sidney, Sir Nicholas Malby, Sir
Richard Bingham, Sir John Perrott, Lord Justice Drury
and Queen Elizabeth I of England. Her name finds its way
into the Sidney, Salisbury and Carew manuscripts, the
Dictionary of National Biography and we have a
fascinating and informative narrative of her life and life-
style in her own replies to the eighteen articles of
interrogatory put to her by the English government in
1593.

The story of Grace O'Malley is 'larger than life', but so
also is the turbulent and eventful age to which she
belonged. The character of Grace O'Malley must be
examined within the context of her time. A century of
exploration and discovery, of wars and intrigue, of
armadas and invasions; of glorious empires at the pinnacle
of their power. The age of Henry VIII, Anne Boleyn,
Thomas Moore, Adrian II, Silken Thomas, Elizabeth I,

Shane O'Neill, Phillip of Spain, Hugh O'Neill, Red Hugh O'Donnell, Francis Drake, Walter Raleigh, William Shakespeare and Edmund Spenser. An age which in Ireland, above all else, saw the final clash and eventual submission of the ancient Irish order, with its hopelessly outmoded medieval structures, to a powerful and persistent sixteenth-century neighbour.

The character of Grace O'Malley, when examined within the confines of this eventful century, emerges not as that of a mythical or legendary figure, but rather as that of an exceptional woman, alive, vital and daring, who lived life to its limits, and who possessed all the requirements necessary for survival in that era. A woman who plied her family trade with all the expertise and enterprise it required, and who above all else put her own interests and those of the small remote domain over which she ruled first, in the never-ending struggle for survival. The last remaining obstacle left to dispel the legendary mists surrounding her name may be due to the fact that she was a woman. A woman 'that hath impudently passed (over-stepped) the part of womanhood' perhaps, but in so doing, she played a unique role in history.

Chapter I

THE O'MALLEYS – TERRA MARIQUE POTENS

Duine maith riamh ni raibhe
D'iabh Máille acht 'n-a mháraidhe;
Fáidhe na síne sibh-sí,
Dine baidhe is bhraithirri.

A good man never was there
Of the O'Malleys, but a mariner;
The prophets of the weather are ye
A hospitable and brotherly clan.

O'Dugan (died 1372)

THE EARLY HISTORY OF THE O'MALLEYS

According to the ancient genealogies of Ireland, the O'Malley clan was descended from the eldest son of the High King of Ireland, Brian Orbsen, King of Connaught, who was killed at the Battle of Dam Chluain, near Tuam, circa A.D. 388. In the *Book of Rights* (Leabhar na gCeart), the O'Malleys are listed as being tributory kings to the provincial kings of Connaught. They were the hereditary lords of the region called the Umhalls (umall, territory) which was latinised as Umallia and later anglicised as the Owels, a territory which comprised the baronies of Murrisk and Burrishoole. The barony of Murrisk was called Umhall Uachtarach or Upper Owel and included the islands of Clare, Inishturk, Caher, Inishbofin, Inishark and the smaller islands in the neighbourhood, including a multitude in Clew Bay. The barony of Burrishoole was

called Umhall Iochtarach or Lower Owel and originally
included Achill. The two baronies were referred to as
'Umhall Ui Mhaille' (territory of the O'Malleys) or the
Two Owels.

The *Book of Rights* lists the rights and tributes to be
paid to the king of Connaught and records that 'the
command of the fleet to O'Flaherti and O'Mali, whenever
he (the king) goes on sea or on high sea'.[1] In respect of the
levys to be paid annually to the king, at his residence at
Cruachan, from the O'Malleys, '100 milch cows, 100 hogs
and 100 casks of beer' was the levy: while the King paid
to the chief of the O'Malleys, in return for his services,
tributes and loyalty, '5 ships, 5 horses, 5 swords and 5
corselets'.

It is not surprising that one of the earliest references to
the territory of the O'Malleys should be associated with
the ascent by St. Patrick of Cruachain Aigle (Mons Aquilae
or Mountain of the Eagle) or Croagh Patrick. In Tirechain's
notes on the life of the saint, which are contained in *The
Book of Armagh,* it is written: 'And Patrick went to
Mount Egli to fast on it forty days and forty nights,
keeping the discipline of Moses and Elias and Christ.
And his charioteer died in Muiresc Aigli — Murrisk — that
is the plain between the sea and Aicill and he buried the
charioteer, Totmael (The Bald One) and piled stones as a
sepulchre and said, "So be it, for ever, and, it shall be
visited by me in the last days". And Patrick went to the
heights of the mountain over Cruachain Aigli, and stayed
there forty days and forty nights.'[2]

The earliest mention of the name O'Malley or Ui Maille
in the Annals appears in 1123, in the Annals of the Four
Masters, where reference is made to the death by drowning
of Teige O'Malley, chief of the clan, near the Aran Islands.
The name appears frequently in the Annals, commenting
on the clan's sailing prowess, tragedies which befell them
on the seas and recording the deaths of the clan chieftains.
For example, in 1127, reference is made to the defeat

Clew Bay

of the Munster fleet by the Connaught fleet, 'chiefly through the superior seamanship of the O'Malleys' and in 1413, Tuathal O'Malley 'on his return home with seven ships and their crews, about the festival of St. Colimcille, a storm arose on the western sea which drove them to the right towards Scotland, where six of his ships with all their crews were sunk . . . Tuathal himself with much difficulty effected a landing in Scotland.'[3] The early history of the O'Malleys reflects the life-style of the Gaelic clans insofar as it records the usual battles, invasions, raids, inaugurations and deaths of chiefs, with, in the O'Malley case, many references to their maritime activities.

THE O'MALLEYS AND THE NORMANS

In 1235 the Norman De Burgos invaded the Umhalls and settled around Umhall Iochtarach, or the barony of Burrishoole, without much opposition from the O'Malleys. Indeed with the emergence of the De Burgos as a ruling force in Umhall Iochtarach, the O'Malley's territory was restricted mainly to Umhall Uachtarach i.e. the barony of Murrisk and the outer islands.

On 10 August 1316, the battle of Athenry (Áth-na-Righ, ford of the Kings) was fought between the forces of Felim O'Connor, king of Connaught, and the Normans of Connaught, in a final desperate attempt by the native Irish to expel the foreigners from the province. The Irish forces were defeated, sustaining heavy losses, mainly through the expertise of the Norman archers. O'Connor's side consisted of a great alliance of Irish kings and chieftains, one of the few occasions when the Irish concerted all their forces against the invader rather than waging futile warfare amongst themselves. The list of those who assembled for battle and those who were slain is comprehensive and it is interesting to note that the names of O'Malley, O'Flaherty and O'Heyne are absent. It is certain that such families of high reputation among the native Irish would have been listed by the annalists if they had been present on the Irish side; the inference is that they either remained neutral or sided with the Normans.

The O'Malleys and O'Flaherties had generally sided with the De Burgos, in opposition to the O'Connors, since the mid-thirteenth century and their absence from the Irish side at this important battle would suggest that their loyalties had remained unchanged. They had co-existed peacefully with their Norman neighbours since the early days of the conquest, separated from other native tribes both by the remoteness of their territories and by wide tracts of land occupied by the Norman settlers. Further evidence of friendliness between the O'Malleys and the Normans is the record in 1330 of the marriage of Edmund De Burgo to Saive O'Malley, daughter of the chief, Dermot.

However in 1342, De Burgo, like many of his fellow Normans, renounced his allegiance to the English crown and assumed the title of the 'MacWilliam Iochtar', or chief of the Burkes of Mayo. Other Norman families in the area followed suit, adopting Irish names and customs: among them Barrett who became MacPadden; Staunton who became MacEvilly; Dexter who became MacJordan; Nangle who became MacCostello; Prendergast who became MacMorris. The O'Malley chief paid no rent or tribute to the MacWilliam, only a 'rising out' or support in times of war and was the only chief in Mayo who retained his rank until the extinction of the title.

THE O'MALLEY TERRITORY

The two Umhalls contain some of the most spectacular scenery in the country, the beauty of which moved William Makepeace Thackeray to write in 1842: 'It forms an event in one's life to have seen that place, so beautiful is it, and so unlike all other beauties that I know of'.[4] The territory is encompassed by the towering peaks of Croagh Patrick to the south, Knockmore on Clare island to the west, the wide expanse of the island-strewn Clew bay, described by Thackeray as 'a miracle of beauty', and Slievemore in Achill and the peaks of the Nephin Beg range to the north. The mainland territory of the O'Malleys to the east comprised some rich farming land around Murrisk, Belclare and Louisburgh, and large tracts of bog, marsh and rough mountain foothills and wooded areas.

Wild animals such as the wolf, deer, fox and badger roamed the more mountainous region, while the black eagle, barnacle goose, swan, woodcock, gannet and cormorant were among the feathered inhabitants. The many rivers and streams of the region were rich in salmon and trout. But it was their extensive sea domain which was the main source of the clan's wealth and survival, with its rich harvest of herring, cod, ling, turbet, pilchard, oysters, scallops, cockles, lobster and crab; fish was the O'Malleys' main trading commodity. In common with most Gaelic clans of the time, however, cattle herds were another source of their wealth and the by-products such as hides and tallow would have been of value both for the clan's own use and for trade.

The Composition of Connaught taken in 1585 states that the O'Malley territory, the barony of Murrisk, consisted of '2 divisions of 36 quarters each called Lorge O'Moyle and Ilane ne Moghere'[5] (The latter is an island in Moher lake situated near the present Westport-Leenane road). In 1607, the Inquisition, taken at Cong, found that 'the barony of Murrske consisted of 80 quarters, whereof 36 are inhabited, the rest waste'.[6] The O'Malley territory of Murrisk stretched along the coast from Cathair na Mart (Westport) west beyond the present town of Louisburgh and included a substantial area of island. Cliara, or Clare island, reposing sphynx-like, guarding the entrance to Clew bay, was the summer residence of The O'Malley and his family and was later to become a more permanent fortress for Grace. It is a lovely island, sheltered to the North by the lofty heights of Knockmore (Cnoc Mór) rising almost 2,000 feet; on the south side are many fine sandy beaches

Grace O'Malley's Connaught, with Galway City Arms

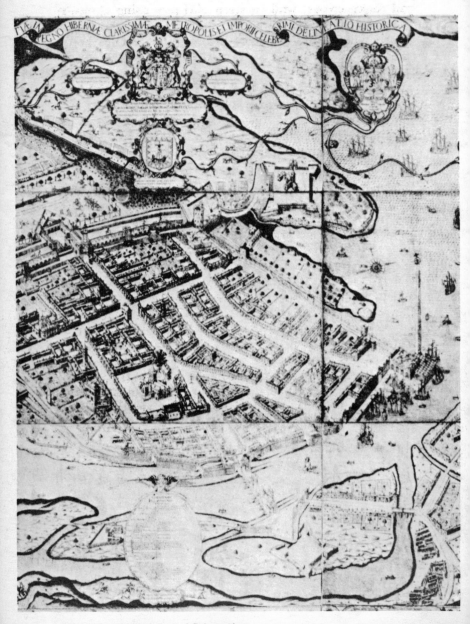

Extract from a 1651 map of Galway city

and rocky creeks, while a steep cliff-face rising abruptly
from the sea guards the north side. Inishbofin (the Island
of the White Cow) originally belonged to the O'Flaherty
family, but was seized by the O'Malleys about 1380. It
lies low in the sea and is surrounded by reefs and minute
islands. To the south of Inishbofin lies Inishark with the
ancient ruins of Teampall Leo (Leo's church). To the
south of Clare island lies the still inhabited island of
Inishturk, or Boar Island, with its wall-like cliffs, and just
east of that is the little island of Cahir or Oilean na
Cathrach (the Island of the Stone Fort), considered a holy
island, where passing boats lower their sail or dip their oars
in reverence. These islands with a multitude of smaller
islands, both in Clew bay and along the indented coastline,
were O'Malley territory.

GALWAY CITY

Galway city was the principal centre of trade in the West
and in the sixteenth century was considered: 'One of the
first emporiums of trade, not only in Ireland, but, with
very few exceptions, in the British Isles'.[7] Many charters
and bye-laws had been enacted, however, by successive
corporations which were prohibitive for non-residents,
especially the Gaelic clans, wishing to conduct trade there.
For example, the exportation of woollens, a mainstay for
many of the Gaelic clans, was prohibited from the port of
Galway. In 1460, the following bye-law had been enacted:

> that ne merchent, ne maryner, ne shipman, should
> unlode, ne transport over the seas, unfremans goods,
> but only fremans, upon paine to lesse the said goods
> or the just value thereof and to forfoyte 100
> shillings.[8]

In 1518 it was enacted

> that no man of the town shall oste or receive into
> their houses at Christmas, Easter, nor no feaste elles,

any of the Burkes, M'Williams, the Kellies, nor no cept else, without license of the major and councille, on payn to forfeit £5; that neither O' ne Mac shall strutte ne swagger thru the streets of Galway.[9]

Judging by these repressive bye-laws, it was imperative that a sea-going clan such as the O'Malleys should make good use of their ability to export and sell their own commodities. And this they had done. For centuries the O'Malleys had sailed the perilous sea-routes to Ulster, Scotland and further afield to Spain and Portugal in their swift and agile galleys, powered by oar and sail, and in the three-masted caravel.

As the Gaelic chieftains gradually regained control over their territories, Irish trade also came to be controlled to a large extent by the native Irish. A petition from a disgruntled English merchant and trader of the time to the English Council 'to have granted unto me and my partners the privilege and only traffic with the lords and people of Ireland for such Irish wares and commodities as is now traded by the Spaniards and Irish men only '[10] is evidence of this.

Irish exports consisted almost entirely of raw materials to both England and the Continent: 'Hides, tallowe, salte beffe in hogsheads, Irisshe coverletts, mantells, and great store of Irishe frises (frieze), both highe cottons and lowe cottons, linine yarone and heringe and salte samon', according to one sixteenth-century list. Fish — either salted or dried — was Ireland's great export commodity at this time. The export of hides and skins closely rivalled that of fish; they were usually exported salted as tanning was not yet well established.

The general outline of export commodities as given in 'The Libel of English Policy'[11] though written in 1436, remains true for the sixteenth century:

I caste to speke of Irlond but a lytelle,
Commodities yit I woll entitelle,

Hydes and fish, samon, hake, herynge,
Irish wollen, lynyn cloth, faldynge, (frieze)
And marternus gode, bene here marchaundyse,
Hertys hydes, and other of venerye,
Skynnes of otre, squerel and Irish are,
Of shepe, lambe, and foxe is here chaffare,
Ffelles of kydde and conyes grete plenté.

Wine was probably the principal Irish import and was obtained direct from France and Spain, Galway being a major port of entry. Salt, necessary for the fishing industry as well as for domestic use was imported 'by all the fishing ports from Wexford to Sligo'.[12] Spices were also imported and alum from England. Fabrics such as damask, canvas, friezes, cotton and a remarkable amount of silk were imported as substitutes for the coarser Irish cloths and were made-up for the households of the Anglo-Irish and Gaelic lords.

The south and west coast ports tended to trade mainly with the Continent and those of the east coast traded with England. The west coast and northern ports traded extensively with Scotland.

THE O'MALLEYS AND THE SEA

The sailing prowess of the clan has been immortalised in legend and song and it is this characteristic that distinguishes them from their contemporaries. Ireland, although an island, has produced very few sea-going families of repute. The O'Flaherties of Connemara, The O'Donnells of Donegal, The O'Sullivans of West Cork are some exceptions. It required a special measure of skill and daring to extract a living from the sea in the sixteenth century along the dangerous west coast. The trade routes to Spain and Scotland were hazardous, weather conditions were harsh, most of their navigational aids were quite basic and there was always the possibility of attack from the ever-present pirates who roamed the high seas. The

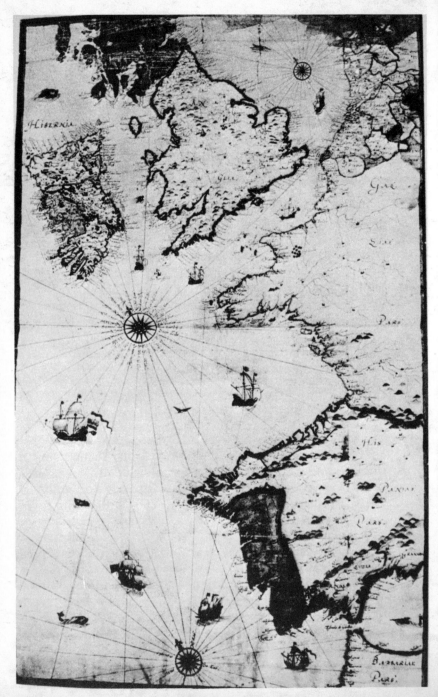

Sixteenth century map of Western Europe

Drawing for a contemporary English galley, showing 54 oars and carrying over 400 men.

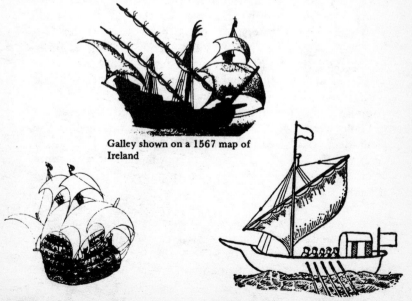

Galley shown on a 1567 map of Ireland

Galley shown on a 1567 map of Ireland

Galley shown on a 1590 map of Ulster (Jobson)

O'Malleys were accomplished and skilful seamen and this contributed significantly to the clan's independence and strength.

This mobility afforded them many advantages over their landbound neighbours, not least of which was the opportunity to see new countries and peoples and observe their customs. The more tangible advantages would of course have been access to foreign markets and to goods and services not available in Ireland. It is reasonable to assume that the O'Malley households contained many items which would not normally be found in other Gaelic establishments of the day; the fabrics and furnishings of Spain would no doubt have replenished many an O'Malley wardrobe and castle; wines from the Continent would have made a welcome change at many meals; the Toledo blade and Coruña-built galley or caravel would have been bargained for and bought in exchange for the cargoes of salted herring, woollens, hides and tallow.

The extent and quality of the O'Malley fleet, at any one time, has never been precisely quantified in any of the many references to it scattered throughout the Annals and the State Papers. It must have been extensive, however, if we are to judge by the accounts of the exploits undertaken by *individual* members of the clan. For example, in 1413, Tuathal O'Malley, 'on his return home with seven ships and their crews'[13] was, according to the Annals, shipwrecked; in 1513 it was recorded that 'Eoghan O'Maile went (with) the crews of three ships against the Cella-Beca (Killybegs);[14] in 1591, Sir Richard Bingham reported that 'Grany O'Maly is preparing herself with some XXte boates in her companie to repaire after them (the Scots)'. [15]

From the records of the Annals and State Papers the galley was the usual type of ship used by the clan. This was a speedy and versatile craft, very suitable for use on the stormy Atlantic, with at least thirty oars plus sail. It could sail, moreover, into narrow or shallow waters where larger vessels could not enter. This type of ship could be used as a cargo, transport or fighting vessel.

The galley originated in pre-christian times, being used by the Phoenicians before 700 B.C. This intrepid, sea-faring race came to Ireland in these wooden vessels powered by rows of oars on each side and a single square sail. The galley continued to be used by the Romans and Greeks and later by the Venetians and Spanish. The term 'galea' was applied to war ships with single rows of oars (as many as 40 on each side) and were much in use between the ninth and sixteenth centuries in Mediterranean waters.

While many descriptions exist of the Irish galley, as used by the O'Malleys, no factual drawing has been preserved. In Francis Jobson's map of Ulster in 1590, there is an illustration of a vessel which according to G. A. Hayes-McCoy 'is clearly intended to be a galley with a sail. . . shown on the map in the sea between Cantyre and Rathlin Island and no doubt it represents one of the craft used by the Scots mercenaries on the voyage between their own country and the Ulster coast'.[16] According to the State Papers however, the galleys used by the O'Malleys would seem to have been much larger and more closely resembled the Spanish or Venetian design rather than the Hebridean. The State Papers record in December 1599:

> There are three very good galleys with Tibbott ne Longe, son to Grany O'Malley, his brother and O'Malley that will carry 300 men apiece. These, if employed by Her Majesty, would do much good in the north, and the O'Malleys are much feared everywhere by sea. There are no galleys in Ireland but these.[17]

In 1601, Captain Plessington, in a dispatch to Sir Robert Cecil, relates that he had a skirmish with an O'Malley galley which was 'rowed with thirty oars and had on board ready to defend her 100 good shot.'[18] In 1602, Sir Oliver

Lambert, regarding his acquisition of a galley for patrol off the west coast of Ireland states: 'I maintain a captain in her and 50 mariners. She rows with 15 oars on a side.' [19] If we consider a galley with fifteen oars aside, allowing 3 to 4 feet between each rower and including a prow and covered stern area, we must think of a vessel of some 80-100 feet in length. For longer trading voyages, the wooden square-rigged caravel/carrack type vessel would have been used. Unlike the galley, this larger ship was propelled by sail only, having three main sails and was widely used for trading purposes during the fifteenth and sixteenth centuries.

PLUNDER AND PIRACY

Although the trading of fish was the primary source of O'Malley income, pillage and plunder would seem to have supplemented the income of some clan members from time to time. In 1396, the Annals of Ulster record 'that Concubar, son of Eoghan Ua Maille, went with a ship's crew, to make an attack in the West of Connaught: the ship was filled by them with the valuables got on (i.e. pirated) that expedition . . .' [20] Later, in 1513, the Annals give a vivid account of a raid by the O'Malleys on Killybegs, County Donegal. They record that Eogan O'Maile went

> with the crews of three ships, against the Cella-beca in the night and the nobles of the country (were) on a rising-out at that time. They raid and burn the town and take many prisoners there and wait on the border of the country during a great storm that over-took them and make a fire in proximity to their ships. And a young stripling of the sons of Brian, son of the Bishop O'Gallcubair and a party of idlers and farm-hands overtake them and they rush on them and there are slain there Eogan O'Maile and five score, or six, along with him and two ships and the prisoners they took are wrested from them, through the miracles of God and Catherine (St.), whose town

Above: the author's impression of an O'Malley galley (drawn by Jarlath Hayes)
Below: Killybegs Harbour, County Donegal. Sixteenth century

A PLAT OF TIE
HARBOR OF CAI
BEG IN THE CO-
VNTIE OF DVN
AGAL

Kildawnet Castle, County Mayo. An O'Malley residence (Commissioners of Public Works)

they profaned previously.[21]

References in the Annals would suggest that piracy and pillage were well established as O'Malley 'pastimes'. Pillage and plunder were common occurrences however and were practised by about every clan and Anglo-Irish family to some degree. The O'Malleys' method differed from the usual, in as much as they mounted an attack usually by ship, confining their activities to the coastal settlements and perhaps by this unorthodox method, securing more notoriety than a common-day cattle rustle for example. The O'Malley strongholds, situated as they were in the sheltering expanse of Clew bay, made fear of reprisal almost non-existent owing to the natural protection afforded by their remote habitat and their own skill as seamen.

MERCENARIES OF THE SEA

The employment of mercenaries was of course, a common feature of Irish warfare. The most renowned of these fighting men were the Gallowglasses or Galloglaigh (i.e. foreign warriors). In Mayo, the Clandonnells or Gallowglass of Mayo, found much scope for their fighting talents and ready employment from both the Irish chiefs and Anglo-Irish lords of the country, not least among them the O'Malley chiefs. If the Clandonnells were the mercenaries of dry land, the O'Malleys, with their galleys were undoubtedly the mercenaries of the sea. It is likely from the many accounts of involvement by O'Malley ships in battles, invasions and skirmishes in various parts of the country, that part of the O'Malley fleet operated on a mercenary basis. O'Malley galleys and crews were eagerly sought after and highly paid for by warring tribes and, judging by the records of the Annals, there was no scarcity of work. In 1413, the Annals of Ulster and Loch Ce record that 'Tuathal Ua Maile with the crews of seven ships went into the Fifth of Ulster (Province of) as a mercenary and he was a year there.' [22] Later, at the turn of the sixteenth century, there is much evidence to suggest that O'Malley men and their galleys were for hire to either the strongest or the wealthiest clients, Irish or English.

THE O'MALLEY POSSESSIONS

The seat of the O'Malley chiefs was at Belclare castle (Dún Béal an Chláir, the Fort at the Mouth of the Plain, i.e. the Plain of Murrisk), and was situated at the mouth of the Owenwee river on the site of an ancient dún or fort. There was also a crannóg or lake dwelling on the island in Moher lake and this was probably the place of refuge for the family and their valuables in times of attack. The family also occupied the castle at Cathair-na-Mart (Fort of the Beeves, i.e. Westport), which was situated near the present Westport House; Carrowmore castle, west of Louisburgh; Kildawnet castle in Achill and the castle on Clare island.

The castles of Clare island and Kildawnet are the only O'Malley castles still in a good state of preservation and, although not the main residence of the O'Malleys, give some idea of the living quarters of the family. The Clare island castle is low-set, irregularly oblong with turret-type chambers projecting on the north-east and south-east. It is three storeys high, and once possessed battlements which were later removed. The three floor-levels, traces of which remain, were plain squares, with recesses and slit oblong windows. The remains of stone passageways and a stairway are evident. This castle, similar to that at Kildawnet is best described as a tower rather than a castle.

The castle on Clare island is situated on a low rocky headland with a splendid view across the bay to Croagh Patrick, while nearby is a fine crescent shaped sandy beach suitable for the beaching of ships and boats. The castle of Kildawnet on Achill Island commands a fine view of the entrance to the Sound.

The O'Malleys, like other Irish families before the Reformation, sustained on their lands monasteries and abbeys maintained by orders of monks, e.g. the Augustinian abbey at Murrisk and the Carmelite (originally) abbey on Clare island.

The abbey at Murrisk was built by the O'Malleys in 1457 for the Augustinian Friars. There are two differing accounts of its foundation. The Rev. Professor F. X. Martin, O.S.A. discovered in Latin notes, held in the Royal Library in Brussels, the following account of its foundation: 'The convent of Murrisk was founded by the most illustrious Lady Maeve Ni Chonchubhair, wife of the most noble Lord Dermot O'Malley, chief of the Owels, commonly called Diarmaid Bacach!' The other version states that on 12 February 1457, Pope Callistus III granted 'permission to Hugh O'Malley, Augustinian friar at the house of Corpus Christi at Banada (County Sligo) to establish a church, friary etc. for Augustinian friars at Leithcarowmursge (the half-quarter of Murrisk) in the diocese of Tuam on land granted by Thady O'Malley, chief of his nation'. [23] It is certain, however, that the O'Malley family was instrumental one way or another in establishing the abbey for the Augustinians.

The abbey at Murrisk is built in late Gothic style and a striking feature is its beautiful and well-preserved east window, with its interlacing bar tracery and its five main trefoil parts, situated over the main altar. Another feature is the turreted south wall. The famous Black Bell of St. Patrick was said to have been kept in the abbey until its suppression.

It is ironic that after the initial account of the foundation of the abbey at Murrisk, nothing of note was recorded about it until the notice of its suppression on 27 March 1574, when Sir Peter Carew mentions, in his dispatch to the Lord Deputy, 'the abbey of Moyriske' as one of the religious establishments in Mayo, 'possessed by Friars or Rebels so as her Majestie hath no commoditee in the same'.

In 1578, Elizabeth leased the lands of the abbey to a James Garvey. It seems that the friars did not disappear from the abbey completely, for in 1635 a chalice, now in Tuam, was presented to them and bears the following inscription: 'Pray for the souls of Theobald, Lord Viscount Mayo and his wife Maeve Ne Cnochoure who had me made for the monestary of Mureske in the year of our Lord 1635'. (Theobold or Tibbot-ne-Long was the son of Grace O'Malley).

The abbey would have figured largely in the lives of the O'Malleys, situated as it was close to the principal residence of the chieftain at Belclare. It would have witnessed the baptisms, marriages and deaths of members of the family. It is likely that Grace was both baptised and married in its chapel and that the remains of her immediate ancestors and descendants lie buried beneath its now roofless walls.

The abbey on Clare island was built by the O'Malleys in 1224. It was originally a Carmelite cell dedicated to the Blessed Virgin, but in later days attached to the great Cistercian house of Knockmoy or *'De Colle Victoriae'*. Like Murrisk it was suppressed about 1574, but it is more than likely that the O'Malleys protected and sustained the monks for many decades more. Inside the chancel on the left-hand wall, facing the altar, is a well-cut undated stone slab. The slab shows a rearing stallion above a helmet and some bar-like objects; a wild boar trippant is in the middle with three bows with arrows affixed and pointed at the boar, while at the right-hand base, a galley features and below that the name 'O'Maille' appears in large letters with the words *'Terra Mariq Potens'* in smaller capitals. A tasselled curtain seems to enfold the entire slab. This stone slab has been assigned to the time of Grace O'Malley, but T. J. Westropp in his book on Clare island, states that its appearance suggests a later date, possibly in the latter half of the seventeenth century. Next to this mural slab is the

Murrisk Abbey, built by the O'Malleys. Drawing c. 1791 by Francis Grose. (National Library of Ireland)

O'Malley tomb, which tradition states is the final resting place of Grace. There still exists evidence of the colour paint-work used to decorate the chapel; traces of scarlet, orange, brown, yellow and deep blue are visible, with figures of a man, a horse, a deer, a harp and other fragments. This paintwork is thought to be the oldest of its kind in the country.

The O'Malley territory bordered Clew bay. To the south was the territory of the Joyces and further south the vast rugged domains of the O'Flaherties with whom the O'Malleys co-existed in relative harmony and peace. The MacWilliam Burkes ruled the territory north of Clew bay and, like the O'Flaherties, maintained peaceful relations with the O'Malleys.

The shelter afforded by Clew bay served as a protection against the elements and the enemy alike. It required both skill and sound local knowledge to navigate a safe passage through the maze of islands, reefs and channels, to Westport or Murrisk. This is perhaps the reason why the O'Malleys were seldom if ever worried by invasions or attacks, especially by the English, whose navigational knowledge of Clew bay and its environs was at best, uncertain. On the open sea, it was a different matter, and skill, strength and daring were required to battle with or evade government ships or Turkish pirate corsairs. The O'Malleys more than held their own and records of sea-battle defeats sustained by them are few and far between.

Stone plaque showing Grace O'Malley's Coat of Arms at the abbey on Clare Island.

Chapter II

IRELAND IN THE EARLY SIXTEENTH CENTURY

THE POLITICAL AND SOCIAL STRUCTURE

Grace O'Malley was born in the earlier part of the sixteenth century, probably in 1530, at the start of an era which was to prove a milestone in the history of Ireland. Up to this time, Ireland had long been, if not the forgotten, then certainly the overlooked colony of the English monarchy. The effects of the Norman invasion centuries earlier were scarcely apparent; Ireland was remote from the centre of English power and administration and by the beginning of the sixteenth century, the country, with the exception of the region bordering Dublin, had been reconquered by the Irish. The native Irish held all Ulster, other than a small region in Down and Antrim, three-quarters of Connaught, the north and west of Munster, the midlands and south Leinster; the customs, laws and language of the native Irish, which had all received a severe blow during the Norman invasion, flourished again. 'So wonderful had those Irish lords encroached into the Pale that afterwards, when the King [Henry VIII]came to the crowne, taking in hand the general reformation of that country, it was found that the English Pale was restrained into 4 counties onlie, viz., Dublin, Kildare, Meath and Louth, and those also not to be free from the Irish invasions'.

Why were the native Irish, who had become so powerful, unable or unwilling to expel the handful of foreigners? The following extract from the 'State of Ireland and Plan for its Reformation 1515' perhaps furnishes the answer: 'There be more than 60 counties, called regions, in Ireland inhabited with the King's Irish enemies, some regions as big as a shire, some more, some less unto a little; where reigneth more than 60 chief captains, whereof some calleth themselves kings, some king's peers, in their language, some princes, some dukes, some arch-dukes, that liveth only by the sword, and obeyeth to no other temporal person but only to himself that is strong; and every of the said captains maketh war and peace for himself and holdeth by the sword and hath imperial juris-diction within his room, and obeyeth to no other person, English or Irish, except only to such persons as may subdue him by the sword'.[2] There was no unifying, central figure around whom the Irish could rally and identify with their regained powers; instead, their energies and resources were wasted on petty warfare with rival chief-tains, a factor which would always be the Achilles heel of Irish resistance, and which now made the true strength of their re-won power very uncertain.

The native Irish, or 'mere Irish' as the English termed them, were not, however, the sole holders of power in the country at this time. There were also the 'King's English Rebels' or the descendants of the Norman invaders, who during the fourteenth century had renounced their allegiance to the English kings and adopted the laws and customs of the Irish; it is often said of them, 'they became more Irish than the Irish themselves'. They too contributed to the weakness of the native Irish by their petty warfare both between themselves and with their Irish neighbours. There were also the great Anglo-Irish lords such as the Kildares in Leinster and the Ormonds in Munster who were in theory loyal to the crown but were in practice independent feudal lords who sometimes found themselves at one with their native Irish and lapsed Norman neighbours.

THE SOCIAL STRUCTURE

Social and political structures in Ireland at this period were

closely interwoven. The social system in the Pale reflected
the English laws and customs. In the regions held by the
old Anglo-Irish families, such as the Kildares and Butlers,
a more feudal way of life existed. The native Irish law, or
Brehon law, was practised by the native Irish and lapsed
Normans throughout the rest of the country. Land tenure,
the method of succession, the dispensing of law and justice
were all accomplished according to the Brehon code. The
Gaelic language was spoken by the majority, with Latin
as a second language, often used in dealings with the
English. Before the Reformation, religion, although at a
low ebb, was one unifying factor.

The Irish clan structure was the centre point of the Irish
social system. It consisted of septs or extended family
groups with powers vested in an elected ruler. The leader
or chieftain was elected by the ruling sept and not by the
right of succession or primogeniture as was the English
custom. The tenure of land through the Gaelic custom
was non-feudal and was accomplished by an arrangement
between the ruling family and his followers which was
suited to the tribal and pastoral nature of Gaelic society.
Cattle herds were numerous and large and were the
principal symbol of wealth and cause of war. There was
little tillage.

In the north, The O'Donnell was called the King of the
Fish (Rí na hEasc); and in the west, The O'Malley issued
licences to Spanish, French and English fishermen to fish
his sea domains.

Gallowglasses of Scottish origin continued to be
employed by the Gaelic and Anglo-Irish alike for the many
disputes over land, cattle, succession or raiding of neighbouring or English strongholds.

Such was the general state of Ireland up to about 1530;
English law had ceased to have any relevance outside the
Pale, which was itself subject to constant attack and
pillage from neighbouring Gaelic clans. Petty warfare was
the regular occurrence, steadily undermining the strength

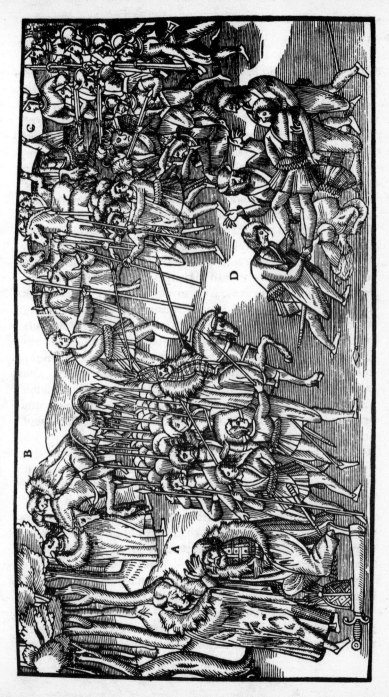

Cattle raid in sixteenth-century Ireland (Derrick, *Image of Ireland*, 1581).

of the Gaelic chiefs. The situation cried out for a strong central figure who could unify the various Irish factions and mould their new power into a strong and effective force. But this was not to be and other than the abortive revolt by the House of Kildare, a unified Irish front, when it did emerge, was too little and came too late.

HENRY VIII AND THE GAELIC ORDER

Grace O'Malley would have been some seventeen years when Henry VIII died. She would have experienced, even in her remote part of Ireland, the winds of political change which had begun to blow across the face of Ireland in the latter half of Henry's reign. With the exception of the ruthless extinction of the House of Kildare in 1537, Henry's policy towards Ireland was one of 'sober ways, politic drifts and amiable persuasions',[3] for the simple reason that a policy of force would have been very difficult to put into effect owing to the strength of the Gaelic chieftains on the one hand, and the slender resources of the English exchequer on the other. This policy of subtle conciliation towards the Gaelic chiefs and Anglo-Irish lords proved to be very effective and was the foundation for the extinction of the old Gaelic order, carried to its conclusion by Henry's successors, especially by his daughter Elizabeth.

From 1529 to 1536, the Reformation in England commanded Henry's attention; the revolt by the House of Kildare, however, directed his gaze across the Irish Sea to his forgotten and neglected colony. Too costly to recover by force, Henry instead created the policy of 'Surrender and Re-grant' to win back his lost kingdom. To implement this policy, Henry had himself confirmed as 'King of Ireland' in 1541. Thus began the new 'Kingdom of Ireland', which was to last until 1800. The policy of 'Surrender and Re-grant' was based on the theory that all lands, held by Gaelic and Anglo-Irish alike, depended on the crown of England. On submission to Henry, the Gaelic chief or

Anglo-Irish lord would receive back his lands in the King's name, agree to rule his lands by English laws and customs, attend parliament and, in return, would receive a title from Henry suited to his rank. Throughout 1541, the most prominent of the Irish chiefs and Anglo-Irish lords submitted to the Lord Deputy. In Leinster, Brian MacGillapatrick submitted and was made Baron of Upper Ossory; Murrough, leader of the great O'Brien clan in Munster was created Earl of Thomond. In Ulster, The O'Neill, regarded as the hereditary King of Ireland, submitted in December 1541 and accepted the title Earl of Tyrone. In Connaught, Ulick Burke, the Upper MacWilliam was created Earl of Clanrickard.

Thus was the start of the Tudor reconquest of Ireland by means of a policy of subtle effectiveness. As the chiefs and lords accepted the terms and titles of the English monarch, so they abandoned the Irish tradition, some more quickly than others, some for as long as it suited their own purposes. It was a triumph for Henry, who at his death in 1547, had by a relatively peaceful, inexpensive, yet highly effective policy extended his power over Leinster and parts of Munster where the Earls of Ormond and Thomond co-operated with the crown in the suppression of the Brehon laws and traditions. In the rest of the country, especially in West Connaught and Ulster, suppression of the native Irish order would take longer, but the machinery for its decline had been firmly set in motion by Henry.

THE CITIES

The provincial towns such as Waterford, Cork, Limerick and Galway, although technically the seat of whatever English power and administration existed, were in practice independent states: 'they elected their own magistrates, excluded the King's judges, contributed nothing to the King's revenue, declared war, and concluded peace without the smallest regard for the Deputy or the Dublin Parliament'.[4] Their power was precarious, however, as the towns and their inhabitants lived in constant fear of attack from their Irish neighbours and kept the high protective walls and gates under constant guard. This fear of attack moved the citizens of Galway to inscribe over the west gate of the city 'from the ferocious O'Flaherties, good Lord deliver us'.

THE PHYSICAL LANDSCAPE

English knowledge of the physical features of Ireland in the early part of the sixteenth century was negligible. The early Tudors possessed no well-defined map of the country and it was not until the latter half of the century, during the reign of Elizabeth, that the art and technique of cartography was brought to a professional standard. Centuries earlier, the Norman invaders had settled on the coastal plains and near the rivers, and had been reluctant to venture into the fastnesses of the inner regions. In the early sixteenth century, the Irish-held areas still lay unmapped and secure behind the natural protection of dense forests and large tracts of bog and marsh. Roads were virtually non-existent and the mountain pass, the forest pathway and the river ford were the key to communication. The English, whose knowledge of the country was negligible, were to find the inaccessible nature of the countryside and also the dampness of the climate, factors contributing to their defeats and indecisive victories over the Irish.

If the Irish-held areas such as the midlands proved inaccessible to the English, it was more difficult still to penetrate the regions of the distant West where any trace of the Norman inheritance had been well and truly submerged by the stronger Irish tradition. 'Until late in the sixteenth century, the English knew as little about West Connaught or its people as did their forefathers'.[5]

The actual mapping of Ireland towards the end of the

century was a major factor leading to the eventual submission of the Gaelic chiefs at the beginning of the seventeenth century. These maps were in themselves symbols of the extension of English administration, deeper and deeper, into once inaccessible and unknown regions, the final bastions of Gaelic law and custom.

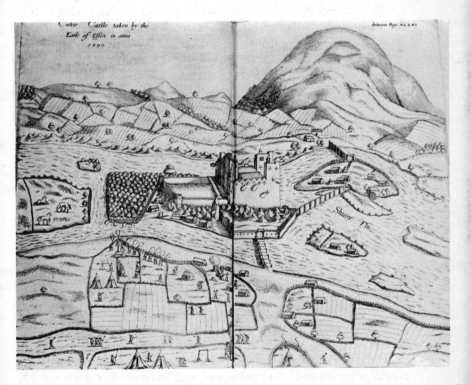

Irish castle (at Cahir) with surrounding houses and fortifications (1599)

A Gaelic chieftain and woodkerne (Derrick, 1581)

The MacSweeney chieftain feasting out-of-doors. A typical 'booley' setting (Derrick, 1581)

Chapter III

GRACE AND THE O'FLAHERTIES

Fortuna Favet Fortibus (O'Flaherty Motto)

EARLY CHILDHOOD

Grace O'Malley is unique as an Irish historical figure of the sixteenth century for she has bequeathed to her researchers interesting documentation of her own life and times. This is contained in her replies to the eighteen articles of interrogatory which the government of Elizabeth I demanded 'to be answered by Grany Ne Malley'[1] in July 1593. Her replies not only furnish the basic facts about her own life but also reflect the social and political conditions of her time.

Grace O'Malley was born into a period which in Connaught, judging by the silence of the Annals, was relatively free from internal disputes or outside invasions. The administration of the English government scarcely touched the region, and a way of life which was old and deep-rooted continued without interference, unaffected by such happenings as the fall of the House of Kildare, Henry VIII's break with Rome or the Reformation.

Grace's father was Owen 'Dubhdarra' (Black Oak) O'Malley, chieftain of Umhall Uachtarach, i.e. the barony of Murrisk. Grace's mother was Margaret, daughter of Conchobhar Og Mac Conchobhair mic Maoilseachloinn, of the sept of Moher O'Malley, a different branch of the same clan.

The earliest reference in the State Papers to Grace's father, chief of the Umhalls, is in 1549, during the reign of Edward VI, when statutes were drawn up by James, Earl of Ormond, and others of the King's Commissioners, in which a list of main regions, counties and the chief Irish of each province was compiled. Under the Connaught heading, in the list of principal chiefs, the name 'O'Mayle of Pomo' appears. This was an interesting misnomer. The word *pomo* in Latin means apple; the Irish word *Umhall,* meaning territory, is pronounced similarly to the Irish word *úll,* apple, and thus the O'Malley of Umhall became the 'O'Mayle of Pomo' in the State Papers.

Grace's father ruled his territory according to the Brehon system, being elected chieftain and receiving the tributes and rents due a chief under this system. At an inquisition taken in Mayo many years later, on 29 July 1607, a successor to the O'Malley chieftainship, Owen O'Malley 'chief of his name and nation' stated that he, as his ancestors before him, 'had chief rents of barley, butter and money out of several lands within the barony of Murrisk and County of Mayo'; that he was 'seised of the castle of Cathir-na-Mart, the castle and island of Carrowmore and numerous other lands and possessions there, in right of tanistry, and that he as chief ought to have, as his ancestors had all fines for bloodshed, all skins of animals killed, or to be killed, within that barony with all customs and other casualities'.[2] The native Brehon customs pertaining to succession, the rights of chiefs and their tenants and the dispensing of laws and justice would seem to have survived in the territory of the O'Malleys long after their abolition in many parts of the country.

Grace had one brother, Donal, nicknamed Donal-na-Piopa (of the pipes), who received mention in the State Papers, and who later resided at Cathair-na-Mart (Westport). Evidence suggests that this Donal was either illegitimate or was Grace's step-brother. In a Bill of Chancery 1606, Grace's son testified that Grace was 'sole heir to the said Margrett'[3] (her mother) and had inherited Margaret's lands in the Owels.

THE GAELIC LIFE-STYLE

The life-style of a Gaelic chieftain's household was geared to out-door activities, a fact reflected in the buildings of the time which were primarily shelters and defences rather than luxurious and stately homes. Owen O'Malley lived in the stone fortress of Belclare with his family and household. Around the outskirts of his castle nestled the thatched mud and stone cabins of his followers, while in front lay the sea, on which his livelihood mainly depended. In the nearby fields grazed the clan's herds of cattle and sheep and the small but hardy Irish horses, used for ploughing and for the few excursions made inland.

Accounts of the way of life in Gaelic Ireland of the sixteenth century were mainly recorded by English travellers who visited the country during this troubled and unsettled era and who were, unfortunately but not surprisingly, biased in their portrayal of the Gaelic customs, manners and practices which differed so much from those of England. They also tended to visit the Gaelic parts of the country during the summer months when, by custom, the chief and his clan left their permanent castle or fortress to live in a temporary summer dwelling called a 'booley' for the purpose of grazing their cattle herds in the uplands. There, the comforts and refinements of their permanent quarters were neglected, given the different and temporary nature of these summer dwellings.

In the summer, Grace's father left his permanent residence at Belclare and with his household left for the 'booley' to graze the cattle herds, but unlike his landbound contempories, to fish and trade as well. This custom of 'booleying' had its origins back in Celtic times and survived in O'Malley territory into the twentieth century, when 'grazing in common was lately found by the Congested Districts Board, in full operation in Clare island, and in re-arranging the land there they wisely left the old custom undisturbed'.[4]

In the seventeenth century while on a visit to the summer residence of Grace's grandson, Murrough-na-Mart O'Flaherty, John Dunton, an English traveller, gives us a glimpse of the lifestyle of a Gaelic chieftain while booley-ing. 'The house was one entire long roome without any partition. In the middle of it was the fire place with a large wood fire which was no way unpleaseing tho in summer time. It had no chimney but a vent hole for the smoake at the ridge'.[5] He was told by O'Flaherty that

they had newly put up this for a "Booley" or summer habitation, the proper dwelling or mansion house being some miles farther neare the sea, and such a one they commonly built everie yeare in some one place or other, and thatched it with rushes. I had sheets and soft white blankets . . . and they assur'd me no man ever gott cold by lyeing on the green rushes, which indeed are sweet and cleene, being changed everie day if raine hinders not.' Dunton was treated well during his stay: 'we had at dinner no less than a whole beef boyl'd and roasted, and what mutton I know not so profewsly did they lay it on the table. At the end where the lady sate was placed an heap of oaten cakes above a foot high, such another in the middle and the like at the lower end; at each side of the middle heap were placed two large vessells filled with Troandor or the whey with butter-milk and sweet milk . . . We had ale (such as it was) and Bulcaan, and after dinner myn host ordered his doggs to be gotten ready to hunt the stagg. He had his horse saddled and one for me too . . . Eighteen long greyhounds and above thirty footemen made up the company.

The O'Malleys were mainly dependent on the sea for their income and much of the clan's work centred on the build-ing and repair of the small hide-covered coracles and

The Gentlewoman of Ireland

The Civill Irish man

The Wilde Irish Woman

The Wilde Irish man

Contemporary sketches of Irish men and women

50

Mulier Hibernica — an Irishwoman.
According to contemporary English
accounts, Gaelic women were 'very
comely creatures, tall, slender and
upright . . .'

Below: watercolour of Irish men and
women by Lucas de Heere.

curraghs and the maintenance of the larger galleys and caravels. Hide-curing, both for export and for their own use, was a major occupation. Fishing was very important and English, Spanish and French fishing fleets, under licence and payment to Grace's father, fished with him for the rich harvest abounding in O'Malley waters. O'Malley fished with net, hook and line both in the sea and on the rivers and lakes, and much attention had to be given to the maintenance and repair of equipment and implements which were held in common by the clan.

Fishing, trading and tending the cattle herds were not their only outdoor pursuits; like the O'Flaherties some of their leisure was spent hunting both the fallow and red deer which abounded in the Umhalls with the help of their great wolfhounds: according to Dunton

> a paire of which kind has been often a present for a king, as they are said to be a dog that is peculiar to Ireland, for I am told they breed much better here than anywhere else in the Kingdom. They were as quiet among us as lambs without any noys or disturbance. I enquir'd the use of them and was told that besides the ornament that they were, they kill'd as many deer as pay'd verie well for their keeping.

He also noted

> on the sides of these hills I wonder'd to see some hundreds of stately red deer, the stags bigger than a large English calfe, with suitable antlers much bigger than I ever saw before .

Falconry was another popular activity and the best falconries were to be found in West Connaught.

Grace's father, Dubhdara, i.e. Black Oak, conjures the image of a tall broad-shouldered swarthy man possessed of great strength, a handsome man, his hair falling to his shoulders and cut in a 'glib' or fringe across the forehead, as was the custom. He dressed in the tight worsted trews

of the time, with a saffron "léine" or shirt with the wide
sleeves falling loosely through the short sleeves of a tanned
leather jerkin. On his feet leather shoes and in his belt a
"Skeyne" or knife. His chieftain's cloak was fastened with
a gold pin at the neck and fell in folds to the ground. He
was a proud man, one of the few Gaelic chiefs never to
have acknowledged the English crown.

Grace's mother, Margaret, as wife of the chieftain
saw to the management of his household and played
hostess to the clan gatherings and social visits by neighbouring chieftains, and their retinues. According to contemporary English accounts, sixteenth century Gaelic
women were

> very comely creatures, tall, slender and upright, Of
> complexion very fayre and cleare skinned but
> freckled, with tresses of bright yellow hayre, which
> they chayne up in curious knotts and devises. They
> are not strait laced nor plated in theyr youth, but
> suffered to grow at liberty so that you shall hardly
> see one crooked or deformed, but yet as the proverb
> is, soone ripe soone rotten. Theyre propensity to
> generation causeth that they cannot endure. They
> are women at thirteene and old wives at thirty . . .
> Of nature they are very kind and tractable . . . [6]

Whether Grace or her mother answered to this peculiar
English description of Gaelic women we do not know.
According to tradition, Grace would seem to have been
dark-haired and of dark complexion. Her mother, as the
wife of a Gaelic chieftain, would have dressed in the
traditional *léine* or smock reaching to the ankles and over
it a long sleeveless dress with a laced bodice, and on her
head a rolled linen headcloth. Grace's mother would have
supervised the work of the women which included spinn-
ing, weaving and dyeing of the clothes worn by the family,
butter-making, baking, the preparation of meals for the
household and the upkeep of the castles and their

contents.

The main meal of the day was taken at evening and it was usual to have a light meal at mid-day. Contrary to many English reports of the time that the entire Gaelic nation existed on buttermilk or 'Bonnyclabbe', the Gaelic diet was quite varied. Porridge or stirabout made of oatmeal flavoured with honey, butter or milk was eaten widely. Venison was a favourite meat, particularly in the West, and mutton and beef were plentiful. Fish was also an important item in the O'Malley diet. Vegetables such as cabbage, onions, wild garlic, leeks and watercress were in use and each family within the clan grew their own supply. Dillisk, eaten with butter, was a delicacy. Hazel nuts were also eaten. Meat was boiled or roasted and a spit *(bir)* made of iron was a very important household implement. Buttermilk was a favourite drink among all classes and was 'wonderfull cold and pleaseing'[7] to quote one English description. The native *uiscebeatha* or whiskey, ale, and wines from Spain and France were drunk. Mead was a drink very much in demand in Ireland and the area that produced it in quantity was regarded as most praiseworthy. O'Malley's kingdom, particularly in the vicinity of Murrisk, was noted for its plentifulness of mead, as the old laudatory expression, 'the mead-abounding Murrisk', suggests.

Meals were served in the chieftain's house on low wooden trestle tables. Meat was placed on large wooden platters from which everyone helped himself by cutting slices with his knife and placing them on wooden plates. Food was eaten with the hands as forks were not in use in either Ireland or England at this time.

In winter, the chieftain's household was entertained from time to time by travelling bards and rhymers who were also the main sources of news and gossip from other parts of the country. These bards were important to the Gaelic structure, for as well as poets and musicians, they were genealogists, historians and chroniclers of current events and were treated with respect in every chieftain's house. Gambling and card-playing were popular pastimes and ones at which Grace clearly excelled — one of her nicknames was Grainne-na-gCearbhach (Grace of the Gamblers). Indeed, one contemporary English account suggests that the entire Gaelic nation was addicted to gambling:

> they nourished a third generation of vipers, vulgarly called carrows, professing (forsooth) the noble science of playing cards and dice, which so infected the public meetings of the people and the private houses of the lords as no adventure was too hard in shifting for means to maintain these. And indeed the wild Irish do madly affect them, so as they will not only play and lose their money and moveable goods, but also engage their lands — yea their own persons, to be held as prisoners by the winner, till he be paid the money for which they are engaged.[8]

The early childhood of Grace centred mainly around the family residences at Belclare and Clare island. Our knowledge of the life of children under the social structure of the old Irish order remains vague, and that of a chieftain's daughter, unknown. Given the unorthodox and unfeminine role Grace was later to adopt, it is likely that from an early age her interests lay, not in her mother's domain of household management, but in her father's world of ships, trade, politics and power; this world must have been the training ground for her future untypical role. These early days, spent on the edge of the ocean, her family's benefactor both in peace and war, no doubt instilled in her a love and aptitude for the maritime life which was to be her career. It is reasonable to assume that she travelled now and then on her father's ships to Spain and Portugal where she would have seen for herself the places and people with whom her family traded.

There is one delightful legend told in explanation of her

nickname Granuaile, Grainne Mhaol (i.e. Bald). According to the legend, as a young child, she begged to be taken on one of her father's ships which was leaving for Spain. She was reminded by her mother that a seaman's lot was no life for a young lady and thereupon, she departed and returned later with her long locks cut as a boy's, much to the amusement of her family who promptly nicknamed her Grainne Mhaol.

It is far more likely, however, that the name 'Granuaile' is a corrupt amalgam of the Gaelic *Grainne Ui (Ni) Mhaille* or Grainne Umhaill (Grace of the Umhalls). There are many variations of the name Grainne Ni Mhaile or Grace O'Malley, in both the Irish and English languages. In Gaelic, Grainne Ui Mhaille, Granuaile and Grania Uaile are the usual versions. In the State Papers in particular, many variations of the anglicised version of her name appear: Grany O'Maly, Grany O'Malley, Grany Imallye, Granny Nye Male, Grany O'Mayle, Granie ny Maille, Granny ni Maille, Grany O'Mally, Grayn Ny Mayle, Grane ne Male, Grana O'Malley, Grainy O'Maly, Granee O'Maillie, Grany ni Maly, Grany ny Mallye.

LORD DEPUTY GRAY VISITS CONNAUGHT

In 1538, when Grace O'Malley would have been about eight, the rumblings of English power and administration drew a little nearer to Western Connaught. After the revolt and bloody suppression of the House of Kildare, Henry VIII's Lord Deputy in Ireland, Lord Leonard Grey, made a tour of the country to see for himself the state of affairs in Henry's neglected domain. On 11 July he arrived in Galway. Lord Grey 'was the first Deputy of Ireland who deigned or rather ventured to approach these western regions'.[9] While in Galway, Lord Deputy Grey received the submissions of The O'Flaherty and The O'Madden; Ulick Burke of Clanrickard, who was The Upper MacWilliam, had submitted earlier.

The submission of these prominent Gaelic and old

Anglo-Irish lords must have signalled the death-knell to
a life of self-determination and relative freedom to the
neighbouring O'Malley and his ally across the bay,
Theobald Burke, The Lower MacWilliam. Up to this time
the affairs of the country or even of Connaught were of
little consequence to the O'Malleys or their immediate
neighbours as long as they were allowed to live free from
interference from either Irish or English. Henry VIII,
however, had set the machinery in motion for the introduction of English administration into his wayward kingdom; The O'Malley, like other Gaelic chieftains, was
faced with the dilemma of standing aloof or submitting
to the English monarch with the likely reward of the
retention of part of his power and privilege as chief. The
O'Malley's remote habitat afforded him the luxury of
thinking it over, and the Lord Deputy departed from
Connaught without his submission. In the meantime,
the fish were plentiful, the work hard but rewarding and
the young Grace grew up in a period free from major
tribulation but with the presence of political and social
upheaval looming ever nearer.

MARRIAGE TO DONAL O'FLAHERTY

Grace was some sixteen years old when she married Donal
O'Flaherty in or about the year 1546. Donal was of the
O'Flaherty clan, which from the middle of the thirteenth
century had ruled the vast, rugged territories of Iar
Connacht and Connemara, separated from the barony of
Murrisk by the fiord-like Killary straits. Like their Norman
neighbours, the O'Flaherties had erected numerous castles
throughout their territory. The most notable of these
castles were Aghanure (the field of the yews); Moycullan
(the plain of Ullin); Bunowen (the mouth of the Owen
river); Ballinahinch (the town of the island); Renvyle or
Currath (Broad Headland) and Doon castle (the fort).
   Donal O'Flaherty was nick-named 'Donal-an-Chogaidh',
(Donal of the Battles) and was the eldest son of Gilleduff

O'Flaherty. His lands included the castles of Bunowen and Ballinahinch. The marriage would have been considered a welcome and good match by both clans. With the exception of one recorded dispute in 1384, the O'Malleys and O'Flaherties had co-existed in relative peace and friendship down through the centuries, a relationship not usual between Irish clans. The sea also bound the two families closer together, being almost as important to the O'Flaherties as it was to the O'Malleys. For the O'Malleys especially, the marriage was a good match for Donal, according to the Gaelic custom, was acknowledged tanaist or heir apparent to Donal Crone, then The O'Flaherty or head of the clan and ruler of all Iar Connacht. Owen 'Dubhdarra' O'Malley was well satisfied for his daughter's future.

LIFE AT BUNOWEN CASTLE

It was at the castle of Bunowen that Grace began her new life as the wife of Donal O'Flaherty. Her husband's other fortress at Ballinahinch was smaller and less spacious than the relatively new castle at Bunowen which was built at the turn of the fifteenth century by Hugh Mór, ancestor of Donal. The castle, little trace of which remains, was a tower-house or fortress with an attached rectangular bawn or enclosure to the north of it. It was situated beside a very narrow and concealed sea-inlet merging with the Bunowen river, four miles to the south-east of Slyne Head. In the time of Grace O'Malley, this narrow tidal inlet provided the only access to this remote castle by small boat or curragh from Bunowen bay and the approach was difficult. The castle was well placed to facilitate the maritime way of life of its inhabitants.

The castle is described by Roderic O'Flaherty, in his 'Description of Iar-Connacht' written in 1684, thus:

Three miles (to the west-ward) of Irrosbeg is the Castle and Manor of Bunowen in Irrosmore. West-

ward of the Castle is Knock-a-Duin (Doon hill) the
third land-mark described by such as sail from the
main. On the East-side of the hill is a harbour for
shipping, and the parish church just by at the hill's
foot. There is an old fortress (Dún) on the top of
the hill which gives the name to the locality of
Ballyndown (Ballindoon), Ballindoon House, Ballindoon parish. St. Flannan, first bishop of Killaloe,
A.D.640, is patron of the parish; and therein his
festival day is kept on the 18th December. On the
West side of the hill (Doon-hill) is a well in memory
of the seven daughters. About two miles hence is
Kennlemy, or the Cape of Slyne-head, the furthest
into the sea and most western point in these parts.[10]

This new home was separated from Grace's father's territory by some of the most wild, rugged and beautiful
scenery in the country. It was bounded to the north-
east by the mighty Twelve Bens (na Beanna Beola) containing the soaring peaks of Bencor (2,336 ft.), Benbawn
(2,305 ft.), Bencailleoghdubh (2,290 ft.), Benderryclare
(2,220 ft.), Bengower (2,184 ft.) and Benlettery (1,904
ft.); to the distant south-east lay the extensive island-
strewn waters of Lough Corrib, while all around were the
moors and stones of Connemara. The lands of Donal-an-
Chogaidh contained a large area of island territory which
included the islands of Imill (Border Island), Omay island
and Inis Lachan or Duck island.

Roderick O'Flaherty furnishes an interesting description of the territory:

The Barony of Moycullan to the east, the half barony
of Rosse lies furthest to the north, the half-barony of
Aran to the South and the barony of Balynahinsey
to the West . . . It is surrounded on the east with
Loughmeasg the isthmus and river of Cong, Lough
Orbsen (Corrib), and the river of Galway, on the
south with the bay of Galway and western ocean,

and with the mountains of Formna more further on
the north. The country is generally coarse, moorish
and mountainous, full of high rocky hills, large
valleys, great bogs, some woods, whereof it had abundance before it was cut. It is replenished with rivers,
brooks, lakes and standing waters, even on the tops
of the highest mountain, on the sea side there are
many excellent large and safe harbours for ships to
ride anchor; the climate is wholesome, soe as divers
attain to the age of ninety years, or hundred and
upwards . . . The greatest number of cattle in this
country is of cows, the soil being for the most part
good only for pasture and grazing and very fertile
of all kinds of herbs. The chieftest product therefore,
and greatest commodity is beefe, butter, tallow,
hides, and of late cheese out of the Isles of Aran;
yet it yields as much corn of wheat, barley oats and
rye, as is enough to sustain the inhabitants, and
furnishes the markets besides . . . Cows and small
sized ponies form the staple stock of Conamara but
sheep are now become more numerous. [11]

Grace must have had little difficulty in adapting to her
new life and surroundings, so similar were they to those
of her father's domain. Becoming mistress of two households may well have proved the most difficult task and
catering for the visits of various members of the extensive
clan who came to consult with her turbulent husband,
Donal, heir apparent to the clan leadership, must have
been a burden to one who wished to be involved not with
household duties, but with the excitement and activity of
a man's world. Her marriage was a fruitful one producing
two sons, Owen and Murrough and one daughter named
Margaret.

The marriage, involving the alliance of two of the most
prominent western families, had every reason to succeed.
But this was not to be. Donal's truculent disposition was

aptly reflected in his nickname 'an chogaidh' (of the battles) and his marriage did not appear to have improved his nature. Political upheaval and intrigue, moreover, were soon to manifest themselves even in the remote kingdom of Iar-Connacht, with unfortunate results for the political aspirations of Donal.

Before this happened, however, an incident which adversely affected Donal's standing as the principal contender for leadership among the Irish of Iar-Connacht took place, in 1549. As both the Annals and Roderick O'Flaherty record, he was implicated in the murder of one Walter Fada (tall) Burke, son of David Burke, later to become The Iochtarach MacWilliam (i.e. chief of the Mayo Burkes), and neighbour and ally of Grace's father. It is recorded that Donal murdered Walter at the instigation of his sister Finola O'Flaherty, Walter's step-mother. Finola wished to secure the succession of the MacWilliam-ship for her own son by David Burke, who was named Richard. (He later became known as Richard-an-Iarainn or Iron Dick, on account of the suit of armour he is said to have worn. It is more likely however that he acquired such a nickname because of the extensive iron mines on his lands around Burrishoole).

The murder was committed at the O'Flaherty castle of Invernan in Moycullen, to the west of Galway, during a visit by David Burke and his son to the territory of his wife's relatives. Eliminating Walter from the list of probable successors to the MacWilliamship, increased the possibility of Finola's own son Richard succeeding his father. Donal's likely gain from murdering Walter was less clear. Finola could have made promises of alliance and co-operation with him when her son would assume the MacWilliamship title and with Donal as probable ruler of Iar Connacht by then, it would have been a very powerful and profitable alliance indeed. There is no evidence to suggest that the Burkes took revenge on either Donal or his sister for the death of their kinsman.

In the meantime Henry VIII had died in 1547 and was succeeded by his son Edward VI. During Edward's short-lived reign, Henry's policy for the expansion of English law and administration continued, advancing deeper and deeper into Irish ruled territories, though not yet touching the outer regions such as West Connaught. The Reformation, whose doctrinal changes Edward attempted to implement in Ireland, made little impact on Gaelic areas. Donal Crone was still The O'Flaherty and Donal-an-Chogaidh continued in the role of the *Tanaist*. In Mayo, David Burke, the father of the murdered Walter Fada, had been elected to the MacWilliamship.

The only recorded disturbance in the area was an incident instigated by Richard-an-Iarainn Burke, who in 1553 raided the territory of the Burkes of Gallen, but was soundly defeated with the loss of 150 of his men and he himself taken prisoner. Again in 1558 this warlike figure induced the Scots, under O'Donnell of Tirconnel, to come into Connaught to plunder the lands of MacMaurice and Lord Athenry, allies of Clanrickard. Clanrickard, however, defeated them on 8 September, killing 700 of the Scots and sending Richard back to Umhall Iochtarach to hatch fresh plots and disorders.

START OF A STRANGE CAREER

And what of Grace? Her life during these years as wife to the turbulent Donal remains a mystery. Her wifely duties as mother, rearing three children, and her duties as mistress of the castles of Bunowen and Ballinahinch, no doubt occupied her for some time. Judging by her character and exploits in later life, however, it is doubtful if she would have been content to undertake a passive role in the events and struggles happening around her. She eventually superseded her husband in his authority over his followers, becoming actively involved in political plotting and intrigue, in both initiating and settling tribal disputes, in fishing and trading and from time to time leading an

attack on merchant ships en route to the port of Galway
and relieving them of their cargo. Galway city had closed
its gates to the O'Flaherties and so, in their eyes, any ship,
English, Irish or Spanish using the port was a justifiable
target for their attack.

When the opportunity arose Grace would swoop out of
the shelter and cover of the islands in swift galleys and
force a lumbering merchantman to a halt. Her men would
scramble aboard and await their leader's command to
pillage and plunder, depending on the outcome of her
negotiations with the ship's captain over a suitable fee for
safe passage to Galway. Then laden with either the agreed
or extracted spoil, Grace and her men would disappear
quickly into the mists and safety of Bunowen. The mayor
and corporation of Galway were powerless against such
attacks and later conveyed their displeasure to the English
Council:

> The continuing roads used by the O'Malley's and
> Flaherties with their galleys along our coasts, where
> there have been taken sundry ships and barks bound
> for this poor town, which (the ships) they have not
> only rifled to the utter overthrow of the owners
> and merchants, but also have most wickedly mur-
> dered divers of young men to the great terror of such
> as would willingly traffic, and let and hindrance of
> their trade no small weakening of Her Majesty's
> Service.[12]

Grace also it would seem took control of the clan's more
peaceful trading missions, sailing far afield to Munster,
Ulster, Scotland, Spain and Portugal to sell the produce
of Connemara at more lucrative and less prohibitive
markets than Galway. Her ships returned laden with the
produce of these faraway places: wines, spices, glass, iron,
rich silks and fabrics, all of which found a ready market
among the Gaelic and Anglo-Irish lords of Connaught who
preferred to purchase from Grace rather than pay the high

import tolls at Galway.

It is difficult to establish why Grace chose this extraordinary way of life. Was there some weakness in her husband's character that forced her to assume the role of leader, or were the qualities of leadership and thirst for power and adventure so much of her being that they became a force within her greater than any of the conventions of her time? Certainly there is evidence in the later life of Donal O'Flaherty that leadership may have been forced upon Grace out of necessity, but there must have been a responding spark in her make-up as a woman for her to undertake such a daunting and dangerous career, at a time when the life of a Gaelic woman was expected to be one of total domesticity.

Across the Irish sea, another woman was also preparing to assume her role in a man's world and she was to excel and be immortalised as the greatest ruler England has ever known. Her impact on Ireland would leave an indelible mark and was to close the door forever on the way of life which Grace knew.

ELIZABETH I

Elizabeth I assumed the English throne in November 1558 and commenced the long and powerful reign which was to end with her ambitions in Ireland realised, the might of Spain shattered and England, for the time being, free from the threat of invasion. For the early part of her reign, Elizabeth was content to continue her father's policy of conquest through conciliatory methods which incorporated the 'Surrender and Re-grant' policy. The coffers of the English exchequer were very low and this method of conquest was less expensive than warfare. The poverty of the English crown was perhaps the key to Elizabeth's many problems in Ireland and the main reason why the conquest took so long to accomplish. The State Papers of the time give evidence of this; their pages are littered with pleas by English generals and administrators serving in

Queen Elizabeth I (National Library of Ireland)

Ireland for financial assistance from the crown.

Ireland was not the only weak chink in England's armour, however; Elizabeth had to keep Scotland passive, maintain a good relationship with France and, above all, keep Spain at arm's length. As the power and ascendancy of Spain became more obvious, the conquest of Ireland took on a new urgency. Elizabeth saw Ireland as the back door to England and she feared that Philip might well make Ireland his base for an attack on England with the Irish rallying to his cause as their new-found leader. It was obvious that 'if the Tudors were to continue to rule England they must rule Ireland as well.' [13] The resistance to this policy which Elizabeth encountered was far greater than that encountered by her father. This was in part due to the efforts she made to implement the conditions of the Reformation. In 1560 the Irish parliament, which represented the anglicised parts of the country only, tried to implement the conditions by legislation with the result that resistance to these measures, both from the Catholic Anglo-Irish and Gaelic Irish, was later to evolve into an all-out resistance to the English conquest in general.

A CLASH OF TRADITIONS

Grace experienced, at first hand, the might of the over-expanding English power which now had eventually pierced the remoteness of Iar-Connacht, drawing O'Flaherty, O'Malley and MacWilliam Burke into its ever increasing net. In 1566 the then Lord Deputy, Sir Henry Sidney, in order to avert possible collaboration by the Galway and Mayo Burkes with O'Neill in the north, 'sent for the Earl of Clanrickard and MacWilliam Eighter (i.e. Iochtar), upon whose Factions all the intestine wars in Connaught hath grown'. [14] Clanrickard and MacWilliam duly came and submitted. Sidney in his description of the meeting states that it was the first time anyone bearing the title of The MacWilliam Iochtar had ever submitted to the crown. Sidney extracted assurances of support against

O'Neill and also settled a quarrel which had arisen between Clanrickard and MacWilliam.

The submission of The MacWilliam was proof that English rule and administration had finally emerged as a force to be reckoned with in Mayo, and The O'Malley, the old ally of The MacWilliam, must have sensed that the time had come when his submission would be requested by the English and, if not forthcoming, his power and privilege as chieftain taken and bestowed on a more receptive member of the clan.

In 1569 such an incident occurred in Iar-Connacht. During the 1560s a young O'Flaherty chief had been making his presence felt in Iar-Connacht. This was Murrough na dTuadh O'Flaherty (Murrough of the Battle-axes, anglicised Murough Ne Doe), who was chieftain of the territory of Gnomore, which formed the northern part of the present barony of Moycullen in County Galway. This O'Flaherty was not of the senior branch of the clan and, therefore, according to the Brehon law, could not be elected chief. He made the castle of Fough (Fuathaidh), situated near the present town of Oughterard. his principal residence and from there he made frequent raids on the territory of Thomond, until Conor O'Brien, the third Earl of Thomond, was forced to march against him in 1560. Murrough evaded him and the Earl was forced to return to Thomond, his expensive and exhausting excursion for nothing. In 1564, the Earl of Clanrickard was also forced to take the field against Murrough, on account of his incursions and raids on the barony of Clare. On this occasion Murrough gave battle and defeated the Earl's forces decisively at Trabane (the white strand), two miles west of Galway. This incident was too serious to be overlooked by the English government. To overcome Murrough by force would prove a costly and possibly inconclusive exercise, considering the remoteness of his territory. On the other hand, if he could be persuaded to become a loyal subject it could prove to be to the government's advantage to have so powerful a Gaelic leader on their side. Murrough, however, was a chieftain of little significance by Gaelic law. To rectify the situation, the Queen, on his submission, pardoned him of all past offences and appointed him chieftain of all Iar-Connacht or in other words, made him The O'Flaherty. In return Murrough promised to 'Observe the Queen's peace, to appear and answer at all sessions within the province when called upon, and to satisfy the demands of all the Queen's subjects, according to justice and equity'.[15] The appointment was in complete contradiction to the Brehon system which had elected Donal Crone as chieftain and Donal-an-Chogaidh as *Tanaist*.

The O'Flaherties of Iar-Connacht became incensed at Murrough for joining forces with the Queen, but especially for presuming to claim jurisdiction over their legitimate chief, Donal Crone, whom they all acknowledged. The peace of Iar-Connacht was shattered and the scene was set for a renewal of tribal warfare, intrigue and double-dealing, by both Gaelic and English alike, as each chieftain, leader or administrator attempted to improve his position and privileges at the expense of friend and foe, aligning himself with whoever was the most powerful or most likely to succeed at playing the game of survival.

Grace, who was about to embark on a career as a person of power and consequence within the province, noted carefully the expulsion of Donal Crone from his rightful position by a force which, although foreign, was apparently far more powerful than the Gaelic chiefs. It demonstrated that from now on one must be apt and able to further one's own interest as the opportunities arose in order to survive the political upheavals, as the Irish and English systems of Government continued to come more and more into conflict under Elizabeth's reign.

FITTON, FIRST GOVERNOR OF CONNAUGHT

In July 1569, Lord Deputy Sidney appointed Sir Edward

Fitton as the first governor of Connaught with the title
of President of the Council. The Council consisted of a
Justice, an Attorney, a Provost Marshall, Sheriffs and
other ranks within the province. The powers of the President were extensive and he, in fact, exercised the powers
and duties of the Lord Deputy when the Lord Deputy was
absent from the province. Fitton was not an ideal choice
of President, being by all accounts an 'ill-tempered,
quarrelsome man, not at all fitted for the delicate duty of
turning Irish into English order'.[16]

In 1570 the Mayo Burkes under the MacWilliam
rebelled. Fitton, with the aid of the Earl of Clanrickard,
Clan Donnell of Leinster, Clan Dowell and others marched
against them and gave battle at Shrule to the MacWilliam
and his allies, who included the deposed O'Flaherty,
Donal Crone and Donal-an-Chogaidh. Both sides claimed
victory but MacWilliam shortly afterwards was compelled to submit and make peace and also to pay 200
marks yearly in rent to the Queen. The MacWilliam died
at the end of the year. During his reign substantial changes
had taken place in his territory. 'When he became the
MacWilliam he was an independent prince, owing but a
nominal subordination and submission to the queen,
whose laws were not yet enforced in his territories. Before
he died the English law was introduced with his consent
and was administered to a small extent by the queen's
representative, independently of him. The Queen's power
afterwards fluctuated, occasionally disappeared, but on the
whole grew steadily'![17]

A period of transition was to follow, in which the power
of the local chiefs was gradually usurped by the Queen's
administrators. The chiefs realised that changes were inevitable, changes which would affect not only their hereditary rights of administering laws and justice within their
own territories, but also affect their rights to their lands
and privileges which existed only so long as it remained
beneficial to English policy in the province. They sought

desperately for any refuge, be it submission to the crown or intrigue with native or foreign powers, in an attempt to make their own positions secure. It was into this scene of uncertainty that Grace embarked making her bid for power.

Chapter IV

GRACE AND THE BURKES

DEATH OF DONAL-AN-CHOGAIDH O'FLAHERTY

With the Queen's replacement of Donal Crone by Murrough-ne-doe, as chieftain of Iar-Connacht, Donal-an-Chogaidh's aspirations to become The O'Flaherty were extinguished. His death must have occurred shortly after this as there is no direct reference to him on record, only references to 'the descendants of Donell Coghie'. According to legend he was killed by the Joyces in revenge for an attack on their territory and for his seizure of the island fortress called Hen's castle *(Caislean-an-Circa)*. This secluded castle on Lough Corrib was a source of constant dispute and warfare between Donal and the Joyces and together with his more usual pseudonym, 'an-chogoidh', he was also referred to as Donal-an-Cullagh 'the Cock' supposedly on account of the great personal courage he displayed while defending this castle. There must have been joy in the Joyce camp, if the legend is correct that they killed him while hunting in the neighbouring mountains, as they imagined that at last the castle was theirs for the taking. They had reckoned without Grace, however, who defended her late husband's castle with such skill and heroism that, just as her late husband had been named 'the Cock' for his courage, Grace acquired the title 'the Hen' for hers, and hence the name *Caislean-an-Circa*, Hen's castle.

Tradition also states that this castle was the scene of one of Grace's exploits some years later. Grace, with a few followers, was besieged on the island fortress, by a strong force of English soldiers from Galway. As the siege con-

Hen's Castle on Lough Corrib. Watercolour c.1790. (National Library of Ireland)

Clare Island castle with barrels of salted fish c.1900 (Lawrence Collection,
National Library of Ireland)

The De Burgo-O'Malley chalice. Silver
gilt, 23cms. high. Inscribed: Thomas de
Burgo et Grainne Uí Malle me fieri
fecerunt. Anno Domini 1494. This
Grainne was an ancestor of Granuaile.

tinued, hope began to fade and conditions inside the castle
became critical. Grace was determined not to surrender
and as the castle roof was lead, ordered her men to strip
and melt it down. The molten liquid was then tipped over
the turrets onto the English besiegers below who beat
a hasty retreat to the mainland, where the siege was continued from a safer distance. With no means of escape, she
despatched one of her men, when darkness fell, to the
Hill of Doon, through the underground passage which
connects the castle to the mainland, to light the beacon
there. She had established a network of beacons along the
coast-line to be used as signals of danger or attack. From
the Hill of Doon flashed the message of her plight and
answering beacons from the Killaries to Clare island
relayed the news. Her fleet put to sea and her followers, on
reaching Lough Corrib, overcame the English and lifted
the siege on Hen's castle.

Grace left her late husband's territory and returned to
her father's kingdom of Umhall Uachtarach. Her future
position in the O'Flaherty country was not very promising;
her husband was dead and her sons were grown men,
involved in securing their own positions in the power
struggle which was to continue in Iar-Connacht. Moreover,
although Grace, as widow of a Gaelic chief, had right to
one third of her late husband's possessions, according to
her later evidence, this was withheld from her. She had
already established herself independently of the
O'Flahertys, securing her own livelihood through 'main-
tenace by land and sea'! She had gathered together a
band of men, numbering 200 by her own admission,
including some of her late husband's followers. She is
reputed to have been very proud of the bravery and
courage of her men and to have said 'go mb'fearr leí lán
loinge de Cloinn Conroi agus de Cloinn Mic an Allaidh
ná lán loinge d'ór'[2] (That she would rather have a shipful
of the Conroy and McAnally clans than a shipful of gold).
As mentioned earlier, Grace had the reputation of being a

gambler and her entourage is said to have habitually
included professional gamblers or dicers known as
'carrowes'. In a poem addressed to Shane O'Dogherty,
the father of Sir Cahir, in the reign of Elizabeth, are the
lines:

> Grainne na gCearbhach do creach
> Is Clann Ghiobúin na ngreadh n-uaibhreach.

> Grace of the Gamblers he plundered
> And the Clan Gibbons of proud steeds.

Grace's father still held the castles of Belclare and Clare
island, her brother Donal was established at Cathair-na-
Mart (Westport). Her family were still in an independent
position for, unlike their neighbours, the O'Flaherties
and the Burkes, they had not submitted to the English
crown and had kept aloof from the Burke rebellion. Grace
made Clare island her stronghold and from there used her
galleys both on errands of trade and piracy. Her exploits
during this period did not go unnoticed by the English
authorities, as later reports on her activities show. For the
time being, however, she was left relatively undisturbed
and continued to be involved in the affairs of the province
and in control of the west coast.

Clare island and Clew bay in general, were perfect
strongholds for her maritime operations; they afforded
a natural protection for her ships and the inaccessible
nature of the area acted as a deterrent to would-be
intruders or pursuers. Her castle on Clare island, in
particular, was very well suited to this type of enterprise.
Its situation afforded her an all-encompassing view of the
wide expanse of water surrounding the island, while the
castle itself could not be noticed by passing shipping from
any great distance, situated as it was:

> by the Atlantic side
> A grey old tower, by storms and sea-wave beat
> Perch'd on a cliff; beneath it yawneth wide
> A lofty cavern, of yore a fit retreat
> For pirates' galleys; altho' now, you'll meet
> Nought but the sea and the wild gull.
> From that cave
> A hundred steps doth upwards lead your feet
> Unto a lonely chamber; Bold and brave
> Is he who climbs that stair, all slippery
> From the wave.[3]

With Clare island in her hands, Grace could monitor every stir, friendly and unfriendly, within the bay; ships en route to Ulster and Scotland or to Munster and Spain were closely watched and were either provided with pilot services or pirated, whichever was considered appropriate at the time. Despite the legends to the contrary, it is likely that Grace was reasonable in her demands of the vessels she boarded, and was careful not to shed blood, if possible, in order to avoid determined government action against her. However, between the pirating of lucrative cargo, the levying of tolls in return for a safe passage through her domain, and the provision of a pilot service for foreign vessels on their way north, her maritime activities were very successful indeed. Her success more than satisfied the needs of the community over which she ruled, and guaranteed her men's loyalty to her as their chieftainess.

About this time, according to legend, Grace and her followers were attending a pilgrimage at the holy well on Clare island on St Brigid's day, when news was brought to her that a foreign vessel had foundered near Achill. The O'Malley boats put to sea in the teeth of the gale in search of survivors and possible plunder, but on arrival it was found that the ship had broken up. Searching nearer the rocks Grace came upon a young man almost dead. She placed him in her boat and brought him back to Clare island where she nursed him back to health. The identification of the castaway varies. According to one legend, he was of Nordic origin; while another states that his name was Hugh de Lacy. One way or another, Grace and her protegé fell in love, but their joy was short-lived, for Hugh as we shall call him, was killed by the MacMahons of Ballycroy whilst deer-hunting on Achill. Grace did not wait long to avenge her lover's death. The MacMahons came on a pilgrimage shortly after the killing to the holy island of Cahir. Grace attacked their boats, cut off their means of escape and then went on the island and slew those responsible for the death of Hugh. From there she sailed for the MacMahon stronghold of Doona castle in Blacksod bay and routed its occupants and installed her followers there. One of Grace's many titles is 'The Dark Lady of Doona' and it perhaps originates in this deed attributed to her in revenge for the murder of Hugh.

The tenacity of Grace in pursuit of her prey, either material or human, is exemplified in the legend regarding Hermit's rock in Clew bay. Some time after the capture of Doona castle, a chieftain of a neighbouring clan, who had been defeated by Grace, took refuge in the church on the tiny island which was inhabited by a holy hermit. Grace in her determination to prevent the chieftain's escape, surrounded the church and waited to starve him out. The chieftain, however, with the aid of the hermit, dug a tunnel out to the steep cliff-face, considered impassable, but by the aid of a rope managed to lower himself down the sheer rock-face to a waiting boat and made good his escape. The hermit, breaking his vow of silence, came out later and informed the waiting Grace that her quarry had escaped and admonished her for attempting to harm one who had obtained sanctuary in his church. Grace's reply was, unfortunately, never recorded.

MARRIAGE TO RICHARD BURKE

The north-eastern side of Clew bay was at this time the only territory not held by the O'Malleys. This fact had not gone unnoticed by Grace, who had already perceived the advantage of controlling a more inland fortress and safe harbour, similar to that of Rockfleet (Carraig-an-Cabhlaigh), for example, whose owner at the time was none other than Richard-an-Iarainn, Iron Dick Burke. About the year 1566, Grace married Richard-an-Iarainn, prominent and powerful chief of the Burkes of Carra and Burrishoole and *tanaist* to the MacWilliam title which was then held by Shane MacOliverus. This was not the first Grace O'Malley-Burke marriage, for in the fifteenth century an ancestor of Grace married Thomas Burke. The celebrated De Burgo-O'Malley chalice, now preserved in the National Museum of Ireland, was made by Thomas and Grace for the abbey of Burrishoole in 1494. The chalice, of silver gilt, weighs 13 ozs. 15 dwts. and is 23 cms. high. It has the following inscription on its base 'Thomas de Burgo et Grainne Ui Malle me fieri fecerunt. Anno Domini 1494'.

Tradition states that she married Richard for a period of 'one year certain', that is to say that if either party wished to withdraw from the alliance, they were at liberty to do so after one year. Marriage and divorce, according to the Brehon laws, were simple and uncomplicated procedures, divorce being a right of both parties. 'In no field of life was Ireland's apartness from the mainstream of European society so marked as in that of marriage . . . Down to the end of the old order in 1603, what could be called Celtic secular marriage remained the norm in Ireland . . . Christian matrimony was no more than the rare exception, grafted on to this system'.[4] When Grace's marriage reached a year's duration, and when she had installed herself firmly in the strategically placed Rockfleet castle, tradition states that on Richard's return from one of his warring missions, she called down to him from the ramparts of the castle 'I dismiss you', meaning that she considered the marriage no longer binding, and as a further blow she informed him that his castle was now hers. However, tradition and legend aside, she married Richard and they did reside for a time in Rockfleet castle as man and wife.

The marriage produced one son, Theobald, born about 1567, who became known as and is recorded in the Annals and State Papers as Tibbot-na-Long or Theobald of the Ships. Tradition is unfortunately our only source of information concerning his nickname. It is said that he was born on board one of Grace's ships on the high seas, on her return from a trading mission. It is also said that the day after his birth, the ship was attacked by a corsair manned by Turkish pirates, who frequently roamed the south and south-west coasts in search of plunder. As the battle raged on deck, Grace's captain came below to report that the battle was going against them but that if she made an appearance on deck her presence might rally the men. 'May you be seven-times worse this day twelve months, who cannot do without me for one day' said Grace, storming onto the deck where she emptied a loaded blunderbuss at the Turks saying 'Take this from unconsecrated hands'.[5] Her men gained new strength and courage from her action and the day was finally won by Grace and her men, who, having captured the corsair and dispatched its crew, sailed homeward for Clew Bay.

ROCKFLEET CASTLE

It was in the bleak tower castle of Rockfleet (*Carraig-an-Cabhlaigh*) that Grace spent much of her life after her marriage to Richard-an-Iarainn. It was here that her son Theobald was reared and from here that she conducted most of her forays on land. Rockfleet castle is situated on an inlet of Clew bay and its ramparts command a fine view of the bay. This stark, square tower, measuring 56 feet in height and comprising four storeys, is in a good state of preservation today. A spiral stone staircase winds past

Carrickahowley or Rockfleet Castle, County Mayo, Grace's principal residence. (Commissioners of Public Works)

Sir Phillip Sidney the poet 'seemed to have been captivated by Grace'.

Sir Henry Sidney (Phillip's father), the Lord Deputy, setting out from Dublin Castle on his tour of Ireland in 1576 (Derrick, 1581).

the lower levels to the main living area on the fourth
floor. The ground floor is earthen while the second and
third floors are of timber. A concave stone ceiling
separates the third and fourth levels. The fourth level,
which has a stone-flagged floor, makes this, the main
living area, completely separate and fireproof, a wise
precaution. A further flight of stairs leads from this main
room to the ramparts above. A curious arched doorway
leading nowhere but to a sheer fifty foot drop to the
rocks below is to be seen on the east wall of the fourth
floor level. It had a less sinister use than one might expect,
being used as a loading bay through which heavy and
bulky goods were hoisted from ground level by means of a
pulley to the main living area. On the south side of the
castle another notable feature is a tiny alcove which
contains a stone privy with an outlet to the tide – a simple
but ingenious feat of plumbing. Loopholes appear here
and there in the walls and were used for the discharge of
musketry. At the north and south angles of the castle are
two projecting turrets while the roof of the building rises
considerably above the parapet walls.

The main living room situated on the top floor measures
20 feet by 18 feet and is some 8 feet high. A large arched
fireplace on the west wall of the room is the focal point
and has two hobs or stone seats on either side. To the right
of the fireplace is a small oblong slit window which allows
the light from the west to penetrate and light up the entire
chamber. To the left of the fireplace is an arched doorway leading from the main stairway. The main window of
the chamber faces north and has a recess of about six feet
in length. The east and south walls also contain slit oblong
windows with small recesses, while in the east wall also is
the arched doorway of the loading bay. There is a curious
loophole in the south wall through which, according to
popular legend, the hawser of Grace's favourite vessel was
run and attached to her bedpost by night as a precaution

lest someone might make the foolhardy mistake of attempting to relieve her of it, and also as a means of communicating an alarm to her apartment in the case of a surprise attack.

The view from the west window and from the ramparts is magnificent and no vessel could enter the inlet without being observed from the castle. It is not difficult to imagine these bare chambers transformed into comfortable living quarters, the stone walls and floors covered with sheepskins, a peat fire blazing in the arched fireplace, throwing a flickering light on the many dark nooks and crannies packed with Grace's implements, spoils and treasures of her trade as well as the more usual household furnishings — a comfortable and adequate stronghold for a sea-queen.

Rockfleet castle was the scene of a dramatic encounter between Grace and the English authorities. At this time Sir Edward Fitton ruled Connaught with iron severity, quelling ruthlessly any incidents of rebellion. His appointment had not deterred Grace, however, and she continued to engage in her maritime activities. So active had she become, especially in harassing ships en route to the port of Galway, that the merchants of the city compelled Fitton to send a force against her. Captain William Martin was chosen to lead a sea expedition of ships and troops. On 8 March 1574, the expedition set sail from Galway and entrapped Grace in her castle at Rockfleet and laid siege. Grace mustered her defences and with her indomitable spirit succeeded on the 26th of the same month, after many days of siege, in turning defence into attack. Captain Martin with his troops and battle-ships were forced to beat a retreat and narrowly escaped capture. It was a resounding victory for Grace, a victory that must have enhanced her position greatly as a leader and a force to be reckoned with.

THE O'MALLEY SUBMISSION

Sir Henry Sidney made a visit to Galway in March 1576 and made an order for the submissions of the Connaught chieftains and lords. Shane MacOliverus was The MacWilliam Iochtar at this time and at first was unwilling to come to Galway but, being persuaded by the Dean of Christchurch, came willingly enough in the end. Of him Sidney wrote, 'I founde MacWilliam verie sencible, though wantinge the English tongue yet understandinge the Lattin; a lover of quiet and Civylitie, desierous to holde his landes of the Quene, and suppresse Irish Extorcion, and to expulse the Scots, who swarme in those quarters and in deede have almost suppressed theirin'. MacWilliam promised Sidney 'to holde his landes of her Majestie, and her Crowne and to pay yerely twoe hundred fyvetie markes sterlinge, and to fynde twoe hundred Soldiers, Horsemen and Footmen, for twoe Monethes by the yere; and to give theirin Foode in that Proporcion . . .' In return MacWilliam received from Sidney, 'his Countrie at my Handes, by Way of Senechallship, which he thankfully accepted. The Order of Knighthoode I bestowed upon hym, whereon he seemed verie joyous, and some other little Trifles I gave hym, as Tokens betwene hym and me, where with verie well satisfied he departed'.[6] It was in theory a complete submission, involving MacWilliam's denial of Gaelic laws and customs, recognition by him that he held his lands subject to the crown and acceptance by him of English demands of payment and by his willingness to accept 'cess', i.e. to provide lodging and food for a specific number of the English army in his territory. For The MacWilliam, it was the most sensible and safest way out at the time. In a strange and unfriendly city, surrounded by the might of English administration and power, was not the place to reveal any misgivings he may have had about the terms of his submission. However, once back safely in his own territory, the articles of submission could be given a wide interpretation.

As well as the submission of The MacWilliam, Sidney received submissions from other Irish chieftains, among them the first recorded submission of The O'Malley. Sidney writes 'O'Maylle came lykewise with him, who is an originall Irishe Man, stronge in galleys and Seamen; he earnestlye sued to hold of the Quene, and to pay her Rent and Service'.[7] The day of reckoning had finally come for The O'Malley. Even when his neighbours and allies had submitted, first The O'Flaherty in 1538 and The MacWilliam later in 1566, he had managed to hold himself aloof. Owen Dubhdarra O'Malley, Grace's father, must have died sometime before this occurrence as the submission was made by Melaghlin O'Malley who had been elected chief. Later in the same year The MacWilliam was officially created seneschal of his territory and Melaghlin was made seneschal of the barony of Murrisk by the Queen. The beginning of the end of the ancient Irish order in the Kingdom of the Umhalls had arrived.

GRACE AND SIR HENRY SIDNEY

On Sidney's departure to Dublin, the sons of the Earl of Clanrickard, Ulick and John, who up to this time had been in custody in Dublin, were released and came back to Connaught to raise yet another rebellion. Sir Nicholas Malby was sent from London to take charge of the affairs of Connaught as Chief Commissioner. He was to prove a more reasonable man than his predecessor, Fitton. In the meantime, the sons of Clanrickard continued their rampage through the province and it was reported that 2,000 Scots had joined them. The MacWilliam adhering to his submission promises, refused to join and his lands were promptly wasted by them. The situation was serious and the English, ever fearful of a major unified rebellion, acted swiftly. Sidney returned from Dublin and marched on Castle Barry (Castlebar) where the castle was held by the sons of Edmund Burke who had joined the rebellion. Although they escaped capture, Sidney took the castle and gave it, in the queen's name to The MacWilliam, who in the meantime had routed the Scots. The sons of Clanrickard, the instigators of the rebellion, surrendered in 1577 but were once again pardoned. Sidney departed for Dublin leaving Malby in charge of a more peaceful Connaught. It was during this visit by Sidney to Connaught that Grace made her first recorded appearance in history when she came, of her own accord it would seem, to meet the Lord Deputy at Galway. Sidney, writing to Sir Francis Walsingham, the Queen's secretary, some years later in a summary of his services in Ireland, recalled this meeting:

> There came to me also a most famous feminine sea captain called Grany Imallye, and offered her services unto me, wheresoever I would command her, with three galleys and 200 fighting men, either in Scotland or Ireland; she brought with her her husband for she was as well by sea as by land well more than Mrs. Mate with him; he was of the Nether Burkes and now [1583] as I hear Mack William Euter, and called by nickname Richard in Iron. This was a notorious woman in all the coasts of Ireland. This woman did Sir Phillip Sydney see and speak withal, he can more at large inform you of her.

The circumstances and reasons for Grace's unrequested submission can only be surmised. It must have been evident to her, as the power and influence of the English crown encroached more and more on the affairs of her country, that the English queen's representatives appeared to wield more power and influence than the highest ranking Gaelic chieftain. In order to survive politically it was imperative to play along with the power of the day. Grace had seen mightier leaders than herself take their *bonnacht* from the Queen and survive. As a Gaelic chieftain's daughter this English prescription might have been a bitter pill to swallow; for Grace, however, with her penchant for gambling both with the dice and with circumstances, for present moment, it was the most profitable remedy. Moreover, her husband, Richard Burke, according to the Gaelic custom, was next in line to the MacWilliamship, but since the present MacWilliam, Shane Oliverus, had submitted in 1576 to the Lord Deputy and had agreed to rule according to English law and custom, it was less certain that Richard would succeed to the title. Consequently, to establish good relations with and make a favourable impression on the English was vital to Grace's future political aspirations. At the same time however, a submission in Galway did not necessarily mean any change either in the politics or activities of her lifestyle in Clew bay, and this remote sanctuary could still be governed according to Grace's own laws and customs. That she was the dominant partner in her marriage to Richard Burke is clearly evidenced by Sidney's observations. She nevertheless made a pleasing and 'a most feminine' appearance, so any preconceived impressions that she was an unattractive, amazon-type creature must be dispelled.

Sir Philip Sidney, the Lord Deputy's son, who accompanied Sir Henry to Galway, seemed to have been captivated by Grace and spoke to her at length. The conversation that took place between this sophisticated Elizabethan knight, courtier, poet, son-in-law of the Queen's private secretary, Sir Francis Walsingham and this extraordinary Irishwoman, has unfortunately never come to light but the meeting must have provided Sir Philip with an incredible story to relate to the English court on his return. Sir Philip, in his notes preserved in the British Museum, does mention one incident which occurred at this time. While in Galway, Sir Henry requested Grace to conduct him and his entourage on a boat trip around the Bay as he wished to view the city's harbour and defences from the sea. Although she complied with the request, business being business, Grace demanded and was given payment by the Lord Deputy for this service.

A period of peace followed Sidney's departure from Connaught and Sir Nicholas Malby seemed to reign as Chief Commissioner with a firm but fair hand. The MacWilliam aided Malby on an expedition against O'Donnell of Tirconnel in Sligo and generally adhered to the articles of his submission.

THE HOWTH INCIDENT

Tradition and legend suggest that it was about this time that Grace made her famous visit to Queen Elizabeth of England, as a proud sovereign queen in her own right, regarding Elizabeth as an equal, and that she was received as such by Elizabeth with all due pomp and ceremony. The legend further relates that on her return from England she landed her ship at Howth and went directly to the establishment of the lord of the area in search of hospitality, as was the Gaelic custom. The gates of Howth castle were locked before her and she was refused admittance, as the lord was at dinner and would not be disturbed. Furious with this disregard for her understanding of the basic principles of hospitality, she stormed from the castle and on returning to her ship came upon and seized the young heir of Howth and sailed for Clew bay. The Lord of Howth, on learning of the abduction, repaired immediately to Connaught and pleaded with Grace for the safe return of his son at any price. Grace, scorning the offer of ransom, demanded that in return for his son, the gates of Howth castle would never again be closed against anyone who requested hospitality and that an extra plate would always be laid at his table. The lord, relieved at the simplicity of the request, readily agreed and was allowed to leave Connaught with his son.

The two related legends, the visit to Queen Elizabeth and the incident at Howth castle, contain some inaccuracies and contradictions. She was indeed received

by Queen Elizabeth but not until 1593 and then under
very different circumstances. The Howth incident is more
difficult to either substantiate or nullify. According to
one seventeenth century historian and genealogist, Duald
Mac Firbis, the incident would appear to have occurred
some sixty years before Grace was born. In his Great Book
of Genealogies, Mac Firbis says of Richard O'Cuairisci
Burk (The MacWilliam (1469-1479): 'This was the very
same Richard who took the Lord of Beann Edair (Howth)
and brought him with him to Tirawley, and there was
nought else required of him for his ransome but to keep
the door of his Court open at dinner time'. However, one
cannot take Mac Firbis' statement as fact without having
regard to the treatment and attitude of Irish sixteenth
and seventeenth century historians and annalists to Grace
O'Malley. While the Elizabethan State Papers and
manuscripts contain numerous accounts of her deeds, her
unusual life-style and her involvement not only in the
affairs of Connaught but also of the country, the Irish
historians and the annalists totally excluded her from their
records. This is quite extraordinary as they record other
quite trivial accounts of places, events and people of the
time. Given that Grace successfully pursued a career so
contrary to the mores of the time, there is reason to
believe that the annalists of the sixteenth and seventeenth centuries, rather than acknowledge that a woman
could dominate in such an unfeminine way, excluded her
completely. This could explain why Mac Firbis trans-
ferred the Howth incident from Grace to Richard Burke.

To the present day, tradition has held steadfastly to its
belief that Grace O'Malley perpetrated the abduction of
the heir of Howth and her name has become so
synonymous with the history of the area that roadways
in present-day Howth are named after her. It is difficult
to ascertain how a western name could have become so
much part of Howth if it had not had its origin in some
explicit episode in Howth's history. However, some

The integrity of tradition: four hundred years later at Howth Castle, the tower gate remains open and an extra place, where the writer sits, is set each day in the dining hall, honouring Grace's request.

Howth Castle in 1801. F. Wheatley. Copy of watercolour original in the castle.

inaccuracies exist; contrary to popular belief, it could not have taken place on Grace's return from the court of Queen Elizabeth because, in 1593, there was no child heir or son of the heir at Howth. It must have occurred during the1570s when the 20th Lord of Howth Christopher St Lawrence, the originator of the incident, was then alive. It is thought likely that the incident occurred in 1576 when Grace put in at Howth, then the principal landing place for Dublin, to replenish her stores for the long voyage around the north coast to Clew bay. She seized the son of the heir, the then Lord Christopher's grandson, also named Christopher, and took him with her to Clew bay and demanded the strange ransom in exchange for the child's return.

Records in the keeping of the present owner of Howth, Mr. Christopher S. Gaisford-St Lawrence, state 'that Lord Howth gave a ring to Grace O'Malley as a pledge on the agreement and that it was preserved in the O'Malley family until in 1795, Elizabeth O'Malley married John Irwin of Camlin (County Roscommon) when the ring moved to the Irwin family. An Irwin son then emigrated to America taking the ring with him. He was a solicitor and later his grandson, John Vesberg, a New York solicitor, had it mounted into a brooch.' The St Lawrence family, down through the centuries, have firmly adhered to the belief that 'The Stealing of the Heir' incident involved Grace O'Malley and the conditions of her ransom demand are enforced at Howth castle to the present day. Francis E. Ball in his book, *Howth and its Owners,* states that 'without direct evidence to controvert it, tradition should not be lightly set aside, and the possibility that an incident such as the tradition relates may have occurred is beyond dispute'. The incident furthermore is so much in keeping with Grace's style and character that, in this instance, what is supposedly a legend is surely a fact.

HER CONQUESTS ON LAND

Grace continued as before, sailing on her missions of trade and piracy, grasping every opportunity as it arose both on land and on sea. In Mayo, it is said that 'she subdued the whole country from Asgalan in the West of Umhall Ui Mhaille to Sliabh Carn, and from Bearna na Gaoithe (the Windy Gap) at Beltraw lake to Ballinrobe', [10] while in other parts of the country, from Donegal to Waterford, there are legends and remains associated with her name. Her name is prominent on the rudimentary map of Ireland drawn by Baptista Boazio for Queen Elizabeth (published in 1599) and is evidence of the extent of her power and involvement in the affairs of the country.

Grace never shunned danger herself. Her courage and her contempt for cowardice is portrayed in an incident which occurred during her attack on the Stauntons of Kinturk castle. According to legend, in the heat of the battle, Grace observed her son Tibbot lose courage and sneak behind his mother to shelter himself from the enemy. Grace in contempt shouted to him 'An ag iarraidh dul i bhfolach ar mo thóin atá tú, an ait a dthainig as? ' ('Is it trying to hide behind my backside you are — the place you came from?'). Whereupon the mortified Tibbot quickly resumed his place at her side. At the end of the day Kinturk castle was surrendered to Grace and the warlike Stauntons subdued. Grace then levied from each family in the district a fine or tribute of a barrel of meal, a pig, and an ox and installed her followers in the castle.

The O'Malley connection with Inishbofin is a long established one and, according to legend, Grace put her own individual stamp on that association. She occupied the old fort, named Bosco's fort, on the island from time to time, and impounded all the sailing craft of the vanquished islanders during her sojourns there. During one of her excursions to the island, two Spanish merchant-ships were sighted making their ponderous way along the rocky coastline on their way north. With visions of booty and treasure, Grace, with a squadron of nine galleys, set sail to intercept them. Her craft succeeded in surrounding and capturing one of the Spanish vessels, while the other, richer in treasure than the one captured, escaped Grace, but fell foul of the elements later and sank off Achill head.

IMPRISONMENT

In 1577, while on an expedition against the Earl of Desmond, whose lands she had plundered, she was captured by him and imprisoned in Limerick gaol, where she was confined for eighteen months. In November 1577, the Earl, as a pledge of his loyalty to the crown, a loyalty which was under suspicion at the time, delivered her up to the then President of Munster, Lord Justice Drury.

Drury, in a letter dated March 1578, communicated the news of Grace's capture to the Lord Deputy and Council as follows:

> Grany O'Mayle, a woman that hath impudently passed the part of womanhood and been a great spoiler, and chief commander and director of thieves and murderers at sea to spoille this province, having been apprehended by the Earle of Desmond this last year, his Lordship hath now sent her to Lymrick where she remains in safe keeping.[11]

Later in the same year, in a letter to Sir Francis Walsingham, the Queen's Secretary, Drury mentions the admirable services performed by the Earl of Desmond in his efforts to prove his loyalty and that in particular he had 'sent in also unto me Granny Nye Male one of power and forces which he took prisoner, which demonstracions of so loyall partes of dealing, argueth in myne opynyon a steadfast hope of his stayed fidelytie'.[12] The privy council were suitably impressed by the Earl's action and wrote in July 1578 to the Lords Justices of Munster:

Gateway to Dublin Castle where Grace was imprisoned in 1578

'We pray you also to signify unto the Earle of Desmond
in howe good parte her Majestie and we take it to understand of his so good and dewytfull behaviour, in making
soche demonstracion of his loyaltie, as you wryte of not
only in words but also in accompaning you at the
Cessions and sending unto you Grany O'Mayle and other
notorious offenders of his countrie'.[13]   At Leighlin on 7
November 1578, Drury again wrote in his despatch to the
Privy Council 'to that place was brought unto me Granie
ny Maille, a woman of the province of Connaught, governing a country of the O'Flaherty's, famous for her stoutness
of courage and person, and for sundry exploits done by
her by sea. She was taken by the Earl of Desmond a year
and a half ago, and has remained ever since with him
and partly in her Majesty's gaol of Limerick, and was sent
for now by me to come to Dublin, where she is yet remaining'.[14]

From Leighlin, Drury sent Grace to Dublin Castle where
she was detained. That Grace's capture was considered by
the Privy Council and Lord Justice Drury to be of such
importance, demonstrates the fact that Grace had certainly made her presence felt and was very active not only
in Connaught but also in Munster. Prison confinement
must have been especially repugnant to Grace, who during
her life had allowed no bonds, neither those of captivity
nor convention, to bind her against her will. The dungeons
of Dublin Castle, which a few short years later were to
be the prison of another Gaelic chief, Hugh Roe
O'Donnell, seldom released any of their convicted tenants
to relate the grim happenings which occurred behind the
dark, dank walls. How Grace managed to evade their
permanent clutches remains a mystery. 'Two of the
M'Shies and Cormock Downe' who were captured also in
Munster and imprisoned with her, were executed at the
castle, but she secured her release and was allowed to
return to Connaught on condition that she would
relinquish her career of 'maintenance by land and sea'.

SIR JAMES FITZMAURICE

Grace arrived back to a Connaught alive with rumours and intrigue about a likely uprising. On the 18th July 1579, Sir James Fitzmaurice, together with the English Jesuit, Dr Sanders, landed in Smerwick on the Dingle peninsula with a small force of Spanish, French and English troops. He had been sent by the Pope to unite Ireland against the 'heretic Queen'. He appealed for aid from most of the Gaelic chieftains and the Earl of Desmond. The O'Flaherties and some of the O'Malleys set sail with a flotilla of galleys to his aid but were forced to retreat back to Clew bay. Before a rising could be even organised, Fitzmaurice was ignobly shot by a sept of the Burkes in Limerick, where he had gone to muster support. Sir John of Desmond assumed the vacant command and after a short time his brother, the Earl of Desmond, Grace's capturer in 1577, finally aligned himself with his brother against the English. The Earl and Dr Sanders wrote to The MacWilliam and to Richard-an-Iarainn, Grace's erstwhile husband, urging them to join in the uprising. The MacWilliam refused but Richard, ever anxious for action, accepted and on the strength of the remoteness of his country 'environed with woods, bogs and mountains, where (to any man's memory) no English Governor hath been at any time, encouraged the Clandonnells to give the English occupation. These Clandonnells were accounted always an invincible people, and the strongest sept of Galloglas in Ireland, and the only men of force in Connaught. Richard in Yeren, having thus won the Clandonnells, joined unto him also the O'Mayles, Clangibbons, Ulick Burke's sept, and certain of the O'Flaherties whereby he thought himself very strong.' [15]

Richard and his forces plundered O'Kelly's and Lord Athenry's territories and Malby set out against him. In his dispatches to the English government, Malby gives a detailed account of his day by day movements against

Richard and his confederates. Malby succeeded in luring the Clandonnells away from Richard and then he took the strong castle of Donamona from Shane McHubert, chief counsellor to Richard, after putting all of its inhabitants to the sword; the resistance began to fade after this. Malby states: 'the 16th [February] I removed to Ballyknock, whither Granny ni Maille and certain of her kinsmen came to me'.[16] Whether Grace had initially sided with and supported her husband in the revolt is not certain. When Richard had lost the initiative, Grace, ever vigilant in promoting and safeguarding her own position, considered it an opportune moment for submission, now that defeat seemed inevitable. Richard, however, with his usual eagerness for action, probably flung himself headlong into the revolt without prior consultation with Grace and without due regard to the obvious consequences. One way or another, Grace, with her ability to read the situation correctly, knew that a voluntary submission now was better than a forced submission later.

On 17 February Malby

removed to Burrishoole, an abbey, standing very pleasant upon a river side, within three miles from the sea, where a ship of five hundred tons may lie at anchor at low water. It hath a goodly and large lough on the upper part of the river, full of great timber, grey marble, and many other commodities of all sides, not without great store of good ground, both arable land and pasture. Specially it hath a very plentiful iron mine and abundance of wood every way. Towards the sea coast there lieth many fair islands, rich and plentiful of all commodities; there cometh hither every year likely about fifty English ships for fishing, they have been before this time compelled to pay a great tribute to the O'Malleys, which I have forbidden hereafter till Her Majesty's pleasure be known. It is accounted one of the best fishing places in Ireland for salmon, herring and all

kinds of sea fish. Richard-an-Iarainn, considering that
the Clandonnells forsook him, and that he was
narrowly persecuted by me and my companions on
all parts of the country, not being able to keep the
field nor make any other resistance, abandoned the
country, and fled into the islands with his Scots and
some gentlemen of his retinue.[17]

Malby waited some days and then moved on to Galway. A
short time later Richard submitted and as was the custom,
gave his 'best pledges'. The revolt was at an end in Mayo
at least, while in Munster it was to continue until 1583.

RICHARD THE MacWILLIAM

On 24th November 1580, Shane Mac Oliverus, The
MacWilliam, died. The Four Masters in recording his death
state that he was 'a munificent and very affluent man, who
preferred peace to the most successful war, and who
always sided with the Sovereign'. [18] Richard-an-Iarainn as
tanaist, according to the Gaelic custom, was to succeed
him. However, Mac Oliverus' brother, Richard Mac
Oliverus, disputed the claim, and Richard-an-Iarainn at
once took up arms, engaged Scots mercenaries and
prepared to defend his rights. The two sons of the Earl
of Clanrickard, Ulick and John, sided with him. Malby,
who was at Athlone, set out to apprehend Richard and
after much negotiating Richard went to him. Malby
relates:

I reassured him, and required the causes of his raising
war, levying forces and paying Scots. He answered
that when MacWilliam died and the Lordship of right
descended to him, sundry friends, and especially the
Earl's son, informed him that I intended to set up his
enemy Richard Mac Oliverus. I told him that he
should have ascertaind my intentions before making
war, and that I was no enemy to him, but my duty
was to uphold every man in his right etc. He said he

Burrishoole Abbey, Newport, County Mayo

really had hoped for mercy, and intended to submit. I said he must deserve it by service to Her Majesty. He said he would do anything in his power. I said, expel the Scots. He asked my help, which I promised.[19]

Richard then aided Malby against the Scots whereupon they 'marched clear out of the province. They were about 600 men, 180 horsemen, 180 targets, 100 long swords, the rest were darts, shot, and gallowglass axes, all as well appointed men as ever I saw for their faculty'. Malby then proceeded to settle the main issue in contention, the succession to the MacWilliamship. He ordered the two Richards to meet and discuss with him. He then appointed Richard-an-Iarainn as The MacWilliam and Richard Mac Oliverus as sheriff. The conditions of the succession were a fine of 100 marks or 100 cows and the banishment by Richard from his country of the Scots mercenaries he had engaged. Richard had secured a good bargain, obtaining the MacWilliamship title at a low cost, in view of his turbulent and often anti-government record. He also got rid of the Scots whom he had employed, without payment of the substantial sum he owed them in wages for their services, as Malby stated in his discourse of the proceedings to the government: 'The charge per annum of M'William's country for the Scots he had engaged was at the rate of £16,800. They had to fly without pay.'

Grace, with Richard installed as The MacWilliam had attained the pinnacle of her power. How instrumental she was in securing the MacWilliamship for her husband has not been acknowledged, but one can be certain that she was very actively involved indeed. She had made a favourable impression in her encounters with the English authorities who, although aware of her illegal activities, were nevertheless impressed by her ability and courage. At the same time, her credibility as a Gaelic leader would not seem to have been adversely affected by this show of co-operation with the English administration, forthcoming only so long as it suited her own purpose. Throughout most of her chequered career she managed to combine effectively with the power of the day, English or Irish, to enlarge and strengthen her own position. With Richard safely installed as The MacWilliam, with the approval of the English government and her Gaelic neighbours, her policies would seem to have been rewarded.

Richard was knighted in September 1581. His reign as The MacWilliam was as turbulent as his career before. Richard MacOliverus, still smarting from his denial of the MacWilliam title, slew some of Richard-an-Iarainn's followers who had been sent into Mac Oliverus country to collect rents. Richard-an-Iarainn retaliated by killing a son of Mac Oliverus and a son of Edmund Burke of Castlebar. Richard Mac Oliverus rose up in arms and sought aid from O'Neill and O'Donnell. The proposed revolt was speedily quelled by Captain Brabazon, one of Malby's captains.

On 28 October, a great gathering of the nobility and leaders in Connaught took place at the governor's residence in Galway. Sir Nicholas Malby, writing to Sir Francis Walsingham stated, that the

> Earl of Thomond, Lord Bryminham, M'William, Richard M'Oliverus, Walter Burke, Murrough ne Doe O'Flaherty, O'Maddin, M'Morris, M'Davy and many gentlemen and their wives, among them Grany O'Mally is one and thinketh herself to be no small lady, are at the present assembled to make a plat for continuing the quietness. [20]

It was an impressive assembly, a gathering of all the principal powers of the province, and yet again, it was Grace who obviously stole the show in this her new role as socialite, a role which for her, must have been very alien indeed. Even in this role she set out to make an impact and from Malby's observations would seem to have succeeded.

Mayo was quiet during the last year of Richard's reign

as The MacWilliam. In January 1583, Sir Nicholas Malby
sent one Theobald Dillon into Richard's territory to
collect rents. Dillon in a dispatch to Sir Francis
Walsingham gives an account of the proceedings:

> I went ther hence to Teyrawlye (Tirawly), the
> forthest part northwards of M'William's contrie, and
> tolde them as afforsayed, who dyd swer they wold
> lyv in like sorte, and payed a C markes due upon
> them this fyv yers paste. I went ther hence towardes
> the plas wher M'William was, who met me and his
> wife Grayn Ny Mayle with all their force, and did
> swer they wolde hav my lyfe for comyng soo furr
> into ther contrie, and specialie his wyfe wold fyht
> with me before she was half a myle nier me. I being
> but a C and fyftie faute men and fyftie horsemen,
> they was contentid to yelde, although they wer afar
> greater in nomber, and gave me for my vitayles xxx
> beavys with wyne and other provision. M'William
> and shee came to Sir Nicholas to agre with hym for
> £600 of areradges due upon their contrie, which they
> thought never to pay. [21]

DEATH OF RICHARD BURKE

On 30 April 1583, Richard-an-Iarainn died, by all accounts
a natural death. The Four Masters in recording his death
state:

> MacWilliam, i.e. Richard-an-Iarainn, the son of David,
> son of Edmund, son of Ulick, a plundering, warlike,
> unquiet and rebellious man, who had often forced
> the gap of danger upon his enemies and upon whom
> it was frequently forced, died.

His was the final appointment to the MacWilliam title
according to the Brehon law of tanistry.

Grace, according to her own testimony, on the death
of her husband 'gathered together all her own followers

and with 1,000 head of cows and mares departed and became a dweller in Carrikahowley in Borosowle (Burrishoole)'. [22] In other words, she immediately laid claim to Richard's property on his death. It was imperative that she act quickly. According to Gaelic custom, the widow of a deceased chieftain inherited one-third of her husband's property but, as Grace later stated in her replies to the articles of interrogatory put to her by the English government in 1593: 'The countries of Connaught among the Irishry never yielded any thirds to any woman surviving the chieftain.' [23] Grace had experienced this before on the death of her first husband, Donal O'Flaherty. This time, however, she established her claim by simply moving herself, her followers and her herds into Burrishoole.

Grace was some fifty-three years old at this time and was still in a position of power in the country. Connaught, however, was soon to be placed in the charge of a new governor under whose severe rule the fortunes of the province and people, and of Grace, were to alter dramatically.

A letter from Bingham with Grace's name in the margin.

A.D·1564·
ÆTATIS·33·
SIR·RICHᴰ
BINGHAM

Sir Richard Bingham, governor of Connaught and arch-enemy of Grace

Chapter V

GRACE AND THE ENGLISH

DEATH OF MALBY

Sir Nicholas Malby died on 3 March 1584. The Annals sum up his contribution to the extension of Elizabethan policy in Connaught: 'There came not to Eirinn in his own time, or often before, a better gentleman of the Foreigners than he, and he placed all Connaught under bondage.'[1] Malby extended the Queen's power and administration throughout the province, culminating in the payment by the lords and chiefs of a rent for their lands, the beginning of a royal revenue for the habitually depleted royal coffers. Legal sessions were regularly held and English law, especially in the trial and punishment of 'malefactors', was enforced. While English laws were not practised throughout the province, Malby had laid the foundations. The Desmond rebellion, which finally ended with the slaying of the Earl of Desmond in the woods of Glenageenty near Tralee on 1 November, did not, after Richard-an-Iarainn's brief involvement, spread to Connaught.

Sir John Perrott succeeded Lord Grey as Lord Deputy in 1584. His instructions from the Queen were, as always, 'to increase the revenue without oppressing the subject, to reduce the army without impairing its efficiency, to punish rebels without driving them to desperation, and to reward loyal people without cost to the Crown'[2] – all in all, an impossible task. Elizabeth's prime difficulty throughout her reign was lack of sufficient revenue, a fact which compelled her to employ penny-pinching and stop-gap measures in the reconquering of her Irish

dominion. With Sir John Perrott came Sir Richard
Bingham, in whose hands the administration of Connaught
was placed on 8 May 1584, about the same time Sir John
Norris was made president of Munster.

Grace at this time was firmly installed at Rockfleet
castle and had once again resumed her career of 'maintenance by land and sea'. Her two sons by her first
marriage, to Donal-an-Chogaidh O'Flaherty, had continued
to oppose the appointment of Murrough-ne-Doe
O'Flaherty by the queen as chief of the O'Flaherties.
Donal Crone, the ousted O'Flaherty, was still alive and, in
spite of Murrough-ne-Doe's assumption of the title, had
continued to exercise and assert his right of chieftainship,
supported by most septs of the O'Flaherty clan, among
them, Grace's sons. Murrough-ne-Doe resolved to subdue
these O'Flaherty septs and compel them to acknowledge
him as their chief. He therefore surprised and captured
the island castle of Ballynahinch. Although a small, in-
significant fortress, it occupied a strategic position in
Iar-Connacht. In 1584, however, Owen and Murrough
succeeded in re-capturing the fortress despite a strong
defence by Murrough-ne-Doe's son, Teige, who retaliated
by plundering their lands and this petty warfare between
the two sides continued for some years. Grace's son
Murrough, however, retained possession of the fortress
until the early seventeenth century.

THE COMPOSITION OF CONNAUGHT

In the meantime, Bingham had commenced his reign as
governor of Connaught. In a letter to the Privy Council,
he stated his plans for subduing Connaught by firm, yet
not oppressive means, 'so that by having too little the
country may not be waste, and by having too much the
people may not rebel. Nevertheless, my meaning is rather
to better their state than to make it worse'.[3] Noble senti-
ments indeed, but unfortunately, owing to his narrow
perception of the situation and his inability to implement

his policies by standing on as few Gaelic toes as possible, his actions did not always reflect his intentions.

At this time the main bone of contention in the province was the practice known as 'cessing'. For many years the authorities had quartered troops and retinues of government officials on the people, often causing great hardship. From the many letters and dispatches in the State Papers, it would seem that the practice of 'cessing' was not favoured by the English either. If 'cessing' was to be abolished, however, a revenue must be raised in its place. This was accomplished by an agreement between the principal chiefs of the province and the Queen which was called the Composition of Connaught. A survey was taken of all the lands in Connaught and a rent of ten shillings per quarter of tillage or pasture land was fixed. The chieftains were also obliged to surrender their rights of exaction of rents and dues according to the old custom and were allowed to retain their lands and castles, succession to be by the English custom of primogeniture instead of the Gaelic custom of election. The Composition of Connaught was signed on 13th September 1585 by all the principal chieftains and lords of the country, including 'Moyaghlyne (Melaghlin) O'Mayle of Belclare, otherwise called O'Mayle chiefe of his name, Teige Roe O'Mayle of Cahairenmart, gent, . . . Owan (Owen) O'Mayle of the same, gent'.[4]

The Composition ordered that The O'Malley 'shall have, hold, possess and enjoy to them their heirs and assigns, not only such castles and lands as belongeth to the name and calling . . . of O'Malley, but also such castles and lands as they or any of them be now justly seized of as their inheritance, the same to descend from each of them to their heirs by course and order of the laws of England'.[5] The Composition was signed by both Melaghlin and Owen O'Malley. Grace's name does not appear among the signatories. Her position as chieftain of Rockfleet castle and the nearby territory, a position she assumed on the

death of Richard-an-Iarainn, was in defiance of both
Gaelic and English law alike. No one of sufficient power
had yet emerged to challenge her.

In Iar-Connacht Grace's sons, Owen and Murrough, were
also allotted their lands according to the regulations of the
Composition. 'And that also Donell Coghye's (Donal-an-
Chogaidh) two sonnes, called Oene and Moragh
O'Flahertie, shall, for their better mayntenaunce of livinge,
have, received and take by letters patentes from her
Majestie to them their heirs and assignes, the Castle of
Bonoune in the barony of Ballynahinsie and 6 quarters of
land with their appurtenaunces next adjoining to the same,
in Ballyndwyn, Mannynemore, Ballycare, and Ballyimon-
gaine, as a free demayne to the said castle, exonerated and
discharged as well of and from this Composition, as also
of and from all other rents, duties and demaunds of the
said Sir Moraghe-ne-doe, Teige ne bullie, and their heires'.[6]
Although Owen and Murrough were named as contracting
parties to the Composition, there is no evidence to show
that, unlike the O'Malleys, they were consenting parties
to it. Their ongoing feud with the principal signatory of
the Composition, Murrough-ne-Doe, may have been the
reason they desisted from signing or, in common with
many other Gaelic chiefs, they may have found the provisions of the Composition repugnant to their beliefs and
ambitions. Although rebellions and complaints, many
stemming from displeasure with the provisions of the
Composition, were to be a frequent occurrence in
Connaught for the next ten years, the abolition of 'cess'
in favour of rents was, for the most part, a relief.

Bingham busied himself implementing the provisions
of the Composition and held the first sessions for Mayo
at the castle of Donamona. A session was also held at
Galway in January 1586 at which seventy people were
hanged, among them many from the chief families of the
province. Disquiet and unrest were apparent amongst the
Gaelic clans, as Bingham persisted in implementing the

Composition to the letter, allowing no leeway for the chieftains to adjust gradually to the new process.

The unrest came to a head in Mayo. Edmund Burke of Castlebar was *tanaist* to the MacWilliam title and after the death of The MacWilliam, there was no indication that Edmund's claim through Gaelic law would be upheld by the English. Edmund, aided by other septs of the Mayo Burkes, rebelled. In February 1586, they fortified the island fortress of Castle Hag in Lough Mask and sent messages for aid to the north. They were also joined by one Richard Burke known as 'Deamhan an Chorrain', (which became anglicised as the 'Devil's Hook', although his nickname is more likely to have originated from the name of the area over which he ruled, i.e. Curraun in Achill). He was the son-in-law of Grace, married to her only daughter, Margaret O'Flaherty. The defenders were later joined by Grace herself.

Bingham attacked the castle with the aid of boats, but was unable to take it and both he and a number of troops were almost drowned in the process. Before he could mount a second attack, the defenders, realising that they would be unable to hold out until help arrived from the north, escaped by boat. Grace, no doubt, was instrumental in effecting their escape. Richard Roe Burke, who had not been actively involved in the revolt, submitted to Bingham who promptly had him, as well as the sons of Walter Fada Burke, tried and hanged. So severe were the reprisals taken by Bingham, that the revolt began to wane. However, friction had arisen between Perrott, the Lord Deputy in Dublin, and Bingham. Perrott was secretly compiling charges against Bingham, accusing him of cruel and unjust practices which had resulted in the revolt in Connaught. Although Bingham in truth had almost quelled the rebellion, Perrott ordered that the remaining rebels be given protection. Some of the rebels returned to their territories and Grace returned to Rockfleet.

The peace did not last for long however. The succession

to the MacWilliam title had yet to be decided, and in June Perrott announced his decision. Edmund was to receive a small part of the MacWilliam lands, while William, son of the deceased Sir Richard MacOliverus, who had been The MacWilliam at an earlier stage, received the greatest portion. Edmund and his followers were incensed at this decision and rose again in revolt. This time he was joined by the Joyces, O'Malleys and Clan Philpin as well as the various septs of the Mayo Burkes.

Meanwhile, Captain John Bingham, brother of the governor, entered Grace's territory in search of booty, especially cattle, a commodity with which she was well endowed. Captain Bingham, aware of Grace's reputation, considered it an opportune time for her to make atonement and arrested her. The result of her arrest is recalled in her own replies to the articles of interrogatory in 1593:

> She was apprehended and tied with a rope, both she and her followers at that instant were spoiled of their said cattle and of all that ever they had besides the same, and brought to Sir Richard who caused a new pair of gallows to be made for her last funeral where she thought to end her days, and she was let at liberty upon the hostage of one Richard Burke otherwise called the Devil's Hook.[7]

This was a lucky escape for Grace, but Bingham did not let her go without obtaining some satisfaction and confiscated her extensive and valuable cattle and horse herds, numbering over 1,000. Her ships once again were her only means of livelihood and salvation.

After some skirmishing, Bingham finally subdued the rebellion of the Mayo Burkes, led by Edmund Burke. At Donamona castle on 30 July, Bingham held sessions and tried and hanged the ninety-year-old Edmund, under Gaelic law the rightful heir to the MacWilliam title. Thus ended the rebellion in Mayo, but in Iar-Connacht in the territory of Grace's eldest son, Owen O'Flaherty, Captain

John Bingham gathered booty and cattle to pay for the expenses incurred by the rebellion. Owen, although married to Katherine Burke and daughter of Edmund Burke of Castlebar, had not taken part in the rebellion. Grace, in her recorded replies, gives a vivid account of Captain Bingham's actions against her son:

> The said Owen, according to Sir Richard's special direction, did withdraw himself, his followers and tenants, with all their goods and cattle into a strong island, for their more and better assurance. There have been sent against the said rebels 500 soldiers, under the leading of Captain John Bingham, appointed by his brother Sir Richard Bingham as his lieutenant in those parts, when they missed both the rebels and their cattle, they came to the mainland right against the said island calling for victuals, whereupon the said Owen came forth with a number of boats and ferried all the soldiers into the island, where they were entertained with the best cheer they had. That night the said Owen was apprehended and tied with a rope with 18 of his chief followers; in the morning the soldiers drew out of the island four thousand cows, five hundred stud mares and horses and a thousand sheep, leaving the remainder of the poor men naked within the island, [they] came with the cattle and prisoners to Bally-ne-heussy [Ballinahinch] aforesaid, where John Bingham aforesaid stayed for their coming; that evening he caused the said 18 persons, without trial or good cause, to be hanged, among them was hanged a gentleman of land and living, called Thebault O'Tool, being of the age of four score and ten years. The next night following, a false alarm was raised in the camp in the dead of the night, the said Owen being fast bound in the cabin of Grene O'Molloy, and at that instant the said Owen was cruelly murdered, having

12 deadly wounds, and in that miserable sort he
ended his years and unfortunate days.[8]

The death of her son, coupled with her own virtual
impoverishment by Bingham, were bitter blows to Grace.
She had incurred the wrath of Bingham who harboured
nothing but resentment for her and detestation of her
unusual activities, and the fact that she was a woman, if
anything, increased his opposition. Sidney, Malby and
even Perrott, on the other hand, had treated her more as a
curiosity than a serious threat to their ambitions in
Connaught, a treatment Grace gladly accepted. She still
retained her galleys, however, but under Bingham's close
scrutiny, she had little room to manoeuvre and when the
pledge of her own good conduct, the Devil's Hook,
rebelled, 'fear compelled her to fly by sea into Ulster, and
there with O'Neill and O'Donnell staid three months;
her galleys by a tempest being broken'.[9] A close association, based on both friendship and business, existed
between Grace, O'Neill and O'Donnell, and it was to them
she fled for sanctuary when conditions in Mayo proved
unfavourable to herself and her enterprises.

In the meantime help from the north had arrived for
the Burkes' rebellion in the form of 1,400 Scots under
Donnell and Alexander, sons of James MacDonnell of the
Isles and Antrim. Having received reports that the Mayo
rebellion had ended, they nevertheless advanced but at
Ardnaree, Bingham aided by the currents of the Moy river,
effectively ended their long march south.

In the north, as in the rest of the country, rumours of a
Spanish invasion were rife and Grace listened and discussed
with The O'Neill and The O'Donnell the chances of
success. Merchants and seamen brought stories of the
musterings of ships, troops and armour in the northern
ports of Spain for an unprecedented attack on England.
Would the attack be mounted through Ireland? Would
Drake's effective patrol of the Spanish coast prohibit an

invasion force from setting sail? The O'Neill and The O'Donnell waited.

The north itself was peaceful enough. Hugh Roe O'Donnell was still a youth and at this time unaware that in a few short months Perrott would have him trapped in the dark dungeons of Dublin castle, the delights of which Grace had already experienced. Tirlough Luineach, the old chieftain of the senior line of the O'Neills, was growing old and weak, while Hugh, the English-educated chieftain and now Earl of Tyrone, was growing in power and ambition. Hugh played a waiting game, cautiously laying plans which in the end would bring him into direct conflict with his one-time benefactress, Elizabeth.

Meanwhile, in Connaught, Bingham was ordered by the Queen for service in Flanders and he departed in July 1587. Sir Thomas Le Strange was appointed in his place and his brother George Bingham appointed later as deputy governor. Peace abided in Mayo when Grace returned to Connaught from Ulster after spending three months with O'Neill and O'Donnell. She took up residence once more in Rockfleet castle. With Bingham her arch enemy out of the way in Flanders, there is little doubt that she made up for lost time and the remains of her depleted fleet once more put to sea in search of sustenance and to recoup her losses. Her cattle and horses having been confiscated by Bingham, maintenance by sea was now her only option for survival.

Grace's youngest son, Tibbot-na-Long (Theobald of the Ships) by her second husband Richard-an-Iarainn, would seem at this time to have been in the custody of John Bingham, possibly on account of his involvement in the Burke rebellion. His youth had been spent as a hostage in the household of Bingham. The Queen in a letter to Sir Richard Bingham later in 1593 refers to this fact when she writes about Grace's 'second son Tibbott Burk, one that hath been brought up civilly with your brother and can speak English'.[10] It is likely that Sir Richard Bingham, as was the custom, had demanded Tibbot as hostage some years previously in order to secure Grace's good behaviour. It was Elizabeth's express wish that the sons of the Gaelic leaders, given up thus as hostages, should be brought up and indoctrinated in the English tradition.

CAPTURE OF RED HUGH O'DONNELL

In September 1587, the 'Eagle of the North', the young Hugh Roe O'Donnell, was lured to his capture and eventual imprisonment in Dublin castle, by Lord Deputy Sir John Perrott. Perrott, in a letter to the Queen, written on 26 September, informs her how it was accomplished and also the reasons for the capture.

> Inasmuch as I found Sir Hugh O'Donnell to be one that would promise much for the delivery of his pledges and the yearly rent of beeves set upon that country, and perform little, and that, in respect he was married to a Scottish lady, the sister of Angus M'Connell, by whom he had a son, Hugh Roe O'Donnell, who ruled the country very much, and thereby not only nourished Scots in those parts, but also certain of the McSwynes (a strong and disordered kind of people there), who have been ready to send aid to any that were evil disposed in your kingdom, as of late they did to Grane Ne Male, to see if they would make any stir in Connaught, I devised to send a bark hence under the charge of one Nicholas Skiper of this city, with certain wines to allure the best of the country aboard, who had such good success as he took and brought hither yesterday in the said bark (without any stir atal) the said Hugh Roe O'Donnell, the eldest son of the galloglasse called McSwyne Fana, the eldest son of the galloglasse called McSwyne Ne Doe, and the best pledge upon the O'Gallahers, all being the strongest septs of Tyrconnell, whereby now you may have (in those

parts) your pleasure always performed . . .

Grace's connection and intrigues with the O'Donnells, suspected by successive governors of Connaught, was now put on record by Perrott to the Queen. The reference in the letter to the latest intrigue between Grace, The O'Donnell and his Scots, possibly related to the large force of Scots who had been sent south to aid the Burke rebellion but who had been defeated on the Moy by Bingham.

A PARDON FROM THE QUEEN

With the English once more in control in Connaught and the Gaelic resistance, for the moment, in tatters, Grace sought and obtained a pardon from the power of the day for both herself and her family. She proceeded to Dublin where she received Queen Elizabeth's pardon from Sir John Perrott. The pardon, preserved in the Calendar of Fiants of Elizabeth, dated 4 May 1588, states:

> Pardon to Grany ny Maly, Shawe Bourke eni Davy Burck widow Tibbott Bourk m'Richarde eneren, gent, Margaret O'Flahertie, daughter of Grany, Morroghe O'Flahertie m'Donill e coggie . . . The pardon not to include murder, nor intrusion into crown lands, or debts to the crown. [11]

The pardon signifies that Grace and her immediate family were much involved in the recent rebellion in Mayo and it contains the only recorded reference to Grace's only daughter, Margaret, who was married to Richard Burke, the Devil's Hook.

THE SPANISH ARMADA

In the spring of 1588 Sir Richard Bingham returned and resumed his duties as governor of Connaught. The rumours of a Spanish invasion became a reality when in July of that year, the invincible Armada set sail for England. Despite its mighty strength, however, after a series of naval battles against the English fleet under the command of Howard and Drake, the Armada lost its crescent-shaped formation and the slow-moving galleons became scattered and easy prey for the fast-moving English warships. The elements then took sides and prevented the Spaniards from either re-grouping or retreating. The unwieldy galleons were driven helplessly along the coast of Scotland, across to Ulster and down along the west coast of Connaught where the terrible winds and rocky headlands took their toll of men and ships.

The hapless Spaniards received a mixed welcome from the Irish. Some months previously, the English government had made it a crime, punishable by death, to aid or protect any of the Spanish invasion forces. The Armada vessels were known to contain untold treasures, the salvage of which appealed to both Gaelic and English alike. Coupled with this, the aims and objectives of the Spanish were not possibly understood by the inhabitants of the more remote regions upon whose coastlines the luckless ships were cast. The O'Neill in Ulster sent provisions and aid to the survivors who had been shipwrecked in his territory and he bitterly reproved The O'Donnell who with some of his clan had aided the English in rounding up the Spaniards. (His son's imprisonment in Dublin castle may have had a possible bearing on The O'Donnell's actions.) On the coast of Mayo, the mighty ship of Don Pedro de Mendoza foundered on Clare Island with 300 men on board. Don Pedro refused to surrender and Dowdarra Roe O'Malley, chieftain of the island at the time, killed all but one, including Don Pedro. It was a terrible slaughter, resulting from greed for the spoils of the shipwreck on the one hand, and out of ignorance and mis-understanding of the reasons for the invasion on the other. The O'Malleys of Clare island were not alone in their treatment of the Spanish. All along the coast the castaways received a similar welcome from most of the natives; others escaped with their lives while the Irish stripped them of their belongings and abandoned them to make their own way. Further up the coast the second in command of the entire Armada expedition, Alonso de Leyva, with his ship the *Rata* with 419 men, was driven by the strong winds into Blacksod bay where the Devil's Hook's son robbed and imprisoned some of the survivors, de Leyva managing after some time to escape to Ulster. A ship of 1,000 tons and fifty-four guns foundered near Grace's territory of Burrishoole. It was reported in London that this was the ship of the leader of the Armada, the Duke of Medina Sidonia, and that he was among the survivors. The English issued orders for his safe conduct, but the rumours proved to be untrue. However, the stricken vessel was indeed rich in treasure of a more mercenary nature.

Grace's attitude and behaviour towards the unfortunate Spaniards is unknown. The lure of treasure and plunder was a way of life to her and there is no reason to suspect that the Spanish cargo would be immune from her attentions. Her attitude to Spanish survivors was another matter. Her family's connections with Spain were long established and her understanding of the Armada's ambitions and aims may have been clearer to one who had spent some time with O'Neill in Ulster. But there was very little she could do to protect or hide the survivors. The ever-vigilant Bingham now gave his undivided attention to the coastline of Connaught. Sir William Fitz-William, the new Lord Deputy, decided that even Bingham's methods were too lenient and he commissioned one Robert Fowle, deputy marshal, to seek out, dislodge and kill any of the unfortunate survivors who had managed to obtain refuge from the Gaelic chiefs. The consequence of harbouring Spaniards was death as the execution of the O'Rourke of Breffni clearly demonstrated later. Grace, with her record by now well established with the authorities and especially with Bingham, must have received very special surveillance and her seagoing excursions would have been closely monitored. In spite of the threats by the English, some of the survivors found permanent refuge and swelled the ranks of some of the Gaelic chiefs such as the Devil's Hook and Sir Murrough-ne-Doe O'Flaherty. The west coast of Connaught took a terrible toll of Spanish lives and Bingham in one of his reports stated 'In my province there hath perished at the least 6,000 or 7,000 men, of which there hath been put to the sword by my brother George and executed, one way or another, about 700 or 800, or upwards'.[12] Thus the remains of the once mighty Armada, the pride of Spain, fell foul of the still more powerful Atlantic with few of the high-masted galleons eventually reaching Cadiz and Coruña.

REBELLION IN CONNAUGHT

The severe treatment used by Fitzwilliam and Bingham against both the survivors of the Armada and the Gaelic chieftains who had sheltered them, gave rise to deep-rooted discontent. Some of the chieftains had refused to hand over the Spaniards and instead employed them in their own ranks of fighting men, and in so doing had, according to the English law, broken the protection given them in respect of past offences. Bingham was in Ulster with the Lord Deputy and, with the English force in Connaught very thin on the ground, the chieftains' discontent erupted into rebellion. Bingham ordered the sheriff for the county, John Browne, with 250 men against the leaders, among whom were the Devil's Hook, the sons of Richard-an-Iarainn by his first marriage, some of the O'Flaherties, Clan Donnell and Tibbot-ne-Long, Grace's son who had been released from custody some time previously.

The sheriff and his troops reached Grace's fortress of Rockfleet on 7 February 1589. Grace's personal involvement in this fresh disturbance is not recorded, but tres-

A contemporary view of the Armada formation

Sir Francis Walsingham, the Queen's Private Secretary in 1577

passers on her domain would no doubt have provoked her into action. Her son-in-law, the Devil's Hook, met the sheriff and objected to his presence in the territory. Browne nevertheless marched on into the heart of the Devil's Hook's territory where he was subsequently attacked and killed. It was a significant success for the Burkes and they were immediately joined by other septs of the clan and by Sir Murrough-ne-Doe O'Flaherty, hitherto defender of the Queen's policy in Connaught, and by William Burke, nicknamed the 'Blind Abbot', who, according to Gaelic custom, was successor to the MacWilliam title, the title which had been dissolved by Bingham.

Grace, perceiving that the coast was clear, to repay the many ills she had suffered at Bingham's instigation, must have grasped the opportunity with alacrity and her galleys provided an efficient method for the transportation of fighting men from Erris to Iar-Connacht as she directed the course of events. The Burkes with Sir Murrough-ne-Doe continued their campaign. Soon after Bingham's return to Connaught the Lord Deputy ordered him to quit hostilities and make overtures for peace. Some interesting notes on the principal participants of the rebellion were compiled by Captain Merbury who served with Bingham's troops. His observations are recorded in the State Papers thus:

> Sir Morogh ne Doe is reckoned above 75 years, the Devil's Hook, Ulick Burke, and Robert O'Maly nigh to 60, Walter Ny Mully (Burke) is exceeding poor, but craftyheaded and bold. Walter Kittough (Burke) is wise enough, but too weak to attain to the MacWilliamship . . . the Blind Abbot was never wise, steady or honest; he doats for age; is very beggarly, overborne by his children. Edmund Burke of Conge . . . . is a very handsome man; always out for fear of the law for killing Ulick Burke of The Neale.[13]

Grace at this time would have been about sixty years of age. During the peace talks that followed, Ulick Burke, Walter Burke and Robert O'Malley came to Galway to negotiate peace terms. They demanded that the MacWilliam title be restored, that no officials should reside in The MacWilliam's territory and that Sir Richard Bingham be removed from the position of governor of Connaught. They promised in return to abide by the law and pay the Composition dues. The Lord Deputy's reply to their demands was: 'They shall have sheriffs and shall not have a MacWilliam.' [14]   The negotiations reached an impasse. The Burkes grew in strength on perceiving the apparent indecisiveness and weakness of the English, as Bingham, still under suspicion by the Lord Deputy, was forbidden to take the field against them. By this time all Mayo had sided with the Burkes and the revolt reached a strength never achieved before. In June, the Burkes and their confederates compiled a Book of Complaints against Sir Richard Bingham, signed by all the principal chieftains of the country. The English submitted their proposals for peace and a tentative agreement was reached. In September seven of Grace's galleys arrived from Ulster with Scots mercenaries. The Scots hoped to get employment in the Burke rebellion, but at this time the Burkes did not require their services. The Scots, in order to supplement their expenses in coming south, helped themselves to 700 of the Burke cattle and departed.

In October, the peace treaty began to wear thin and the Burkes once more reiterated their demands for the restoration of the MacWilliam title. On 15 October, in open defiance of the government, they elected and installed William Burke, the 'Blind Abbot', as the new MacWilliam. The Burkes were now masters of Mayo and parts of Galway and the rebellion was going from strength to strength. The Queen wrote her displeasure to the Lord Deputy at the restoration of the MacWilliam title as the Burkes had now acquired a central figure around whom the rebellion could revolve. Bingham at this time had been cleared of almost all the charges brought against him and his trial in Dublin was almost completed. In December he was acquitted and in January 1590, aided by the Earls of Thomond and Clanrickard, he moved swiftly against the Burkes through Castlebar and on to Barnagee, where the Burkes attacked but were routed. Bingham moved on to Tirawley where in a skirmish, the Blind Abbot was injured. In Erris, Bingham plundered all before him. He arrived in Burrishoole on 16 January where he proceeded to kill indiscriminately men, women and children. The rebellion lost its momentum under Bingham's ruthless but effective tactics and on 23 January, Edmund, son of Richard-an-Iarainn (by his first marriage), was sent by the Burkes to sue for peace. According to the State Papers, the cost of the Burke rebellions to the English Exchequer was: 'War against Burkes in 1586 — £1,476.3s.4d.; War against the Burkes in 1589-1590 — £3,296.17s.6d.'.

Grace, however, aware or unaware that peace was made, continued her own war as Bingham reported to Sir Francis Walsingham in a letter dated 21 April: 'Immediately after the peace was concluded, Grana O'Malley, with two or three baggage boats full of knaves, not knowing that the peace was made, committed some spoil in the Island of Arran upon two or three of Sir Thomas le Strange's men, to the value of 20 marks, which she did by the persuasion of some of the O'Flahertys. Presently after that Sir Thomas was dead . . . Richard Burk, the Devil's Hook, hath Grana O'Malley in hand till she restore the spoils and repair the harms'.[16] Once again it was her son-in-law who went guarantor for Grace's good conduct.

The degree of involvement by Grace in this rebellion has not been recorded in any detail. With her son, son-in-law and stepson actively involved, there is little doubt but that her galleys were busy along the coast. Her support and aid for the compilation of the Book of Complaints against Bingham is certain, in view of his treatment of both

herself and her family. Bingham's great severity in dealing
with those who in his estimation broke the law, and his
uncompromising attitude to the rights and wrongs of the
newly introduced English system in Connaught afforded
no opportunity for the Gaelic inhabitants to adjust to a
system which was alien to their very nature. For Bingham,
conciliation was not the means to attain the end, suppression in his eyes was the only effective way of
implementing the Queen's policy. Although many of the
charges brought against Bingham, both by the Burkes
and by his own fellow administrators, especially Perrott
and Fitzwilliam, were later found to be false, it was his
methods rather than his intentions which were more often
in question.

In her determined opposition to Bingham, Grace went
so far as to attack her own son, Murrough O'Flaherty of
Bunowen in Iar-Connacht. Murrough had sided and aided
Bingham against Grace and the Burkes in the latest
rebellion. Grace, incensed at the idea of her own son
daring to oppose her, sailed into Bunowen with her galleys,
plundered and spoiled Murrough's lands, killed some of
his followers in the process and departed for Clew bay,
her galleys laden with the spoils of attack. In September
1593, Bingham in a letter to the Queen's private secretary
concerning this incident states:

> his [Murrough's] aforesaid Mother Grany (being out
> of charety with her sonne for serving her Matie:)
> manned out her Navy of Gallyes and landed in
> Ballinehenchie where he dwellethe, burned his Towen
> and spoiled his people of their Cattayle and goods
> and murdered 3 or 4 of his men which offered to
> make resistance .

Bingham cites this incident hoping 'to gyve your honour
Knowledge of her naughty disposicion towards the state'.
After this incident there is little heard about Murrough
for some years. It was not so much the fact that her son

aligned himself with the English; Grace would not hesitate herself if the outcome was to be to her advantage, but that her son would align in opposition to her and in aid of her arch enemy Bingham, that was too much for any mother to accept, so that son had to be taught a lesson.

GRACE AND THE SCOTS

In June 1591 Grace went into action again when some of her Burke relations, among them the sons of the Blind Abbot, were killed in a conflict with some Scots mercenaries who had come down by boat from Ulster in search of booty. Bingham, in a dispatch to the Lord Deputy dated June 1591, described the occurrence:

It maie please your honour sithence my last unto your Lordship as towchinge the arryval of the Scottes on the coastes of Irrys [Erris], I have latelie received credible advertisements from thence that in the con- flicte betwixte the Burkes and them, twoe of the Blind Abbettes sonnes are slaine the one outerighte and the other being sore hurtt dyed sithence; there is likewise one of the O'Malies, one of the Walter ne Mullie's brothers, one of the Clangibbons, and divers others of the Burkes being badd and notorious knaves, dyed sithence, the said encounter, being sorelie hurte at the instant. And likewise twoe of the principall leaders of the Scottes are slaine, with many others onn there syde, and howe happie channces this is, in the cutting of those badd members, to there generall quiet and tranquilities of this province. I referre it to the relacion of all such as knoweth the same. The Scottes are nowe departed from hence towards there owne country. And Grany O'Maly is preparing herself with some XXte boates in her companie to repaire after them in revendge of her countrie men, and for the spoil they committed in those partes, which I am contented to tollerate, hoping that all or the moste parte will take their journey towardes heaven, and the province ridd of manie badd and ill disposed persons.[17]

The ironic humour of Bingham, suggests that she still continued to be a thorn in his side. He is more forceful in his condemnation of her later in 1593 when he refers to her as 'a notable traitoress and nurse to all rebellions in the Province for 40 years'.[18] Bingham likewise was perhaps the single biggest obstacle Grace had encountered. Under Sidney and even the dour Fitton, she had managed to rule her ocean territory and to continue to ply her trade virtually unopposed. Under Bingham's administration, however, west Mayo became less remote from the centre of English rule and administration, until eventually the power and influence of the English government pierced its armour of obscurity, revealing all its secrets. But time as well as Bingham had caught up with Grace. She was now over sixty years of age and the possibility of continuing her active and remarkable sea-life was rapidly fading. Bingham had robbed her of her livelihood on land, so the grim fortress of Rockfleet must have appeared grim indeed to an ageing woman whose only means of support must be extracted from the tempestuous Atlantic, which through the advent of old age, would become more and more difficult for her to master.

A letter from Bingham with Grace's name in the margin.

Chapter VI

GRACE AND QUEEN ELIZABETH I

HUGH O'NEILL IN ULSTER

Hugh O'Neill in Ulster was cautiously preparing for war. He had allied himself with the other leaders of the province and especially with the young Hugh Roe O'Donnell, who in 1592 had escaped from Dublin Castle. In 1593, O'Neill persuaded the ageing chieftain, Turlough, to acknowledge him as The O'Neill and in effect as the hereditary chief of the entire Gaelic kingdom of Ireland. Emerging at last from the debris of Gaelic discord and division was a strong central figure to whom the various Gaelic clans and families might yet rally for leadership. O'Neill continued his outward show of loyalty to Queen Elizabeth, while in his dispatches to the Spanish court he outlined his plans for another Spanish invasion, this time with Ulster as the target.

A STRUGGLE FOR SURVIVAL IN CONNAUGHT

In 1591, the principal leaders of the Mayo Burkes died. These were Walter Kittagh, chieftain of the Tirawley Burkes and Walter Mully who was murdered by his own nephew. The Blind Abbot was no longer in contention for any position of power and Grace's son, Tibbot-ne-Long, emerged as the principal leader of the Burkes, a position which he held onto grimly until his death in 1629. Tibbot had inherited Grace's instincts for survival in the ever-changing political field and he frequently played both sides of the coin to secure and advance his own position.

His rise to power as the principal leader of the Mayo
Burkes was in itself contrary to the old Gaelic system, as
many members of the clan, especially the sept Ulick, were
his seniors and under the old system would have been
elected leader. Owing to the power vacuum created by
Bingham among the Burkes, Tibbot, like Grace, seized his
opportunities as they arose and acted accordingly. He
married Maeve, the daughter of O'Connor Sligo and his
territory included the baronies of Carra, Gallen and Owle
Iochtarach.

Despite the political intrigue and activity which would
normally have attracted her attention Grace was at this time
involved in a struggle for survival, not in the political
sense but for her very existence. Bingham had reduced
the Burkes, formerly relatively wealthy and powerful, to
abject poverty and Grace, despite her more independent
means of securing a livelihood, had not escaped either.
Of the Burkes, Bingham wrote in September 1592: 'I find
the Devil's Hook's son, Edmund mac Ricard an Iarainn
and Tibott mac Rickard an Iarainn to be men of no possessions, or to have any goods so much as half a dozen cows
apiece'. Although exaggerated, Bingham's observations
nevertheless demonstrate the depth to which these Burkes,
Grace's son among them, had fallen. It was imperative then
that they align themselves with a power, Gaelic or English,
that could restore their lost wealth and position. Grace's
own dominance over the western coastline and in particular over her own sanctuary of Clew bay had been
penetrated at last by English shipping, as Bingham related
in the same dispatch: 'At Burrishoole we met our shipping,
and so continued there two nights altogether. The shipping had done great service for the same had cleared all their
islands'.[1] Bingham's penetration and subsequent domination of Grace's sea domain, resulting in the virtual
impounding of her fleet, was the single greatest setback
Grace had encountered. She was never fully to recover
from it.

Despite all the problems she had encountered in running the gauntlet with the English authorities, she had always contrived to retain control of her fleet and her immediate coastline. This freedom of movement enabled her to remain a leader longer than most in the province. But now her very survival rather than a reassertion of her former position of power was her immediate concern, while her ambitions for power might yet be realised in the person of her son Tibbot-ne-Long. Bingham had been instrumental in reducing her to her present state, a state in which he intended she should remain; the only recourse open to her now in her efforts to secure the restoration of her rights and those of her family was to appeal to a higher authority than Bingham, and that authority appeared to Grace to be the Queen of England.

PETITIONS TO QUEEN ELIZABETH

Record of Grace's first letter to Elizabeth appears in the State Papers for July 1593. It is written in English and addressed 'To the Queen's Most Excellent Majesty'. It is thought unlikely that the letter was written by Grace herself. Similar to many of the Gaelic chieftains, her knowledge of the English language would have been very limited, as Latin was usually used for communications with the English authorities. It is an interesting letter and, although the letter of a supplicant seeking favours, the courage, daring and cleverness of Grace is manifest in its tones. The letter begins in the usual tones of a petition:

> In most humble wise showeth unto your most excellent Majesty; your loyal and faithful subject Grany Ne Mailly of Connaught in your Highness realm of Ireland that where by means of the continual discord stirs and dissention which heretofore long time remained among the Irish especially in West Connaught by the sea-side, every chieftain for his safeguard and maintainance and for the defence of

his people, followers and country took arms by
strong hand to make head against his neighbours, who
in like manner constrained your highness fond subject
to take arms and by force to maintain herself and her
people by sea and land the space of forty years past.[2]

In the opening lines Grace immediately establishes her
version why she had been 'forced' to conduct a campaign
for the past forty years against what had in reality, been a
flaunting of English authority, details of which she was
aware had already been brought to Elizabeth's attention,
especially by Bingham. Grace's excuse for her behaviour
hints at the inability of Elizabeth's Connaught governors
to cope with the situation, thus *forcing* her to assume
her career of 'maintenance by land and sea'. It was a bold
bid to secure a pardon without necessarily repenting of the
crime.

Her letter continues with a brief résumé of her life and
marriages to O'Flaherty and Burke and of her present
destitute circumstances. She asks the Queen to settle some
maintenance on her from her late husbands' estates. 'In
tender consideration whereof and in regard of her great
age, she most humbly beseeches your majesty of your
princely bounty and liberality to grant her some reasonable maintenance for the little time she has to live.' She
requests the Queen to accept the surrender of her two
sons, Murrough O'Flaherty of Bunowen and Tibbot-ne-
Long, so that in keeping with the Queen's policy, they
might hold their lands of the crown and that this might
also apply to her relations, Walter Burke Fitztheobalt
and Shane Burke MacWilliam.

Then, despite her 'great age' and the 'little time she has
to live' and mindful that Bingham has put a stop to her sea
exploits, she seizes this opportunity of reinstating herself
in her old role as leader of her fleet and followers when
she asks the Queen

to grant unto your said subject under your most
gracious hand of signet, free liberty during her life
to invade with sword and fire all your highness
enemies, wheresoever they are or shall be, without
any interruption of any person or persons whatsoever.

In other words, by the Queen's specific command, she
would be above Bingham's control and free to pursue
her activities on land and sea as before, but this time
with her Majesty's approval. It was an ingenious plan.

THE ARTICLES OF INTERROGATORY

Whether the Queen was intrigued by the tones and content
of the petition or whether the details she had to hand,
from the dispatches of her governors concerning the activities of Grace, made her want to know more about this
extraordinary women, we do not know; but during July
1593 eighteen articles of interrogatory were dispatched
by Burghley, the Queen's private secretary, to be answered
by Grace. The set of questions and the answers provided
by Grace are preserved in the State Papers,[3] with observations in the margin in Burghley's handwriting, and they
not only furnish an informative résumé of Grace's life, but
also throw some light on the political and social conditions
of west Connaught at the time. The eighteen articles are
listed numerically and are answered in similar order by
Grace. Questions 1 to 7 deal with her family, her two
husbands, her sons and her first husband's relationship to
Sir Murrough-Ne-Doe O'Flaherty. Questions 8 to 10 deal
with the position of widows in the Gaelic community.

In question number 8 she is asked: 'If she were to be
allowed her dower, or thirds of her husband's living, of
what value the same might be of'. Grace replied: 'The
countries of Connaught among the Irishry never yielded
any thirds to any woman surviving the chieftain whose
rent was uncertain, for the most part extorted, but now
made certain by the composition and all Irish exactions

merely abolished.' A chieftain who ruled according to the Brehon code had little fortune and few possessions to bequeath to his wife. Owing to the uncertainty of the chieftain's income, he usually died in debt, with his wife suffering the consequences. (Some clans did make provision for the widow of a chieftain in the form of what was known as a 'canebeg' (*caine beag*) or tax which was levied off the chieftain's territory.) Owing to the prevalence of divorce, a woman when she married according to Grace's testimony 'for fear of the worse' received from her husband securities for the return of her dowry if he divorced her and re-married. With divorce the right of both parties, however, Grace neglected to mention the consequences for the chieftain, if his wife decided to divorce him as she is reputed to have done to Richard-an-Iarainn!

The remaining queries and answers, numbers 11 to 18, deal with an account of her life since the death of Richard-an-Iarainn in which Grace recalls the circumstances leading to her seizure by Bingham and her narrow escape from hanging, her flight to Ulster and her pardon by Perrott in Dublin; queries on the relationship of other Burkes to her late husband and queries relating to the identification of various Mayo townlands and castles.

Grace's replies are always guarded and she concentrates on the aspects and events of her life which would be considered least objectionable to the English government. She wisely neglects to mention her plundering exploits by land and sea, her part in the Burke rebellions, her collusion with O'Neill and O'Donnell and the Scots mercenaries. Her deft replies were in fact a match for the sophistication and intrigue of the British government and demonstrate her astute mind and her daring; these qualities had yet to face their ultimate test in face-to-face negotiations with one who also possessed such qualities in abundance — Elizabeth, Queen of England.

MISSION TO ENGLAND

Shortly after her replies had been sent to London, an incident occurred which added new urgency to Grace's petition. Bingham arrested her son, Tibbot-ne-Long, on charges that he had communicated with Brian O'Rourke of Breffni and had offered to raise Mayo in support of the Ulster chieftains, on condition that O'Rourke would keep Bingham busy in Breffni and so direct his attention away from Mayo. Coupled with this, her brother, Donal-na-Piopa of Westport, had also been imprisoned by Bingham some months past for the murder of some English soldiers. Thus, Grace had now to petition the Queen not only on her own behalf, but on behalf of her family and relations, and, judging by her correspondence to both the Queen and Burghley, she had now assumed the role of matriarch of the Burkes and the O'Malleys in placing their cases before the Queen, without any objections from the chiefs of the respective clans.

Bingham's latest actions against her family spurred Grace into action. The time for written petitions was past. During late July 1593, Grace, accompanied by her first husband's old adversary, Sir Murrough-ne-Doe O'Flaherty, set sail from Connaught for London in an effort to obtain an audience with the Queen. Legend relates that Grace captained one of her own ships for the voyage and this is quite likely. The south coast and the channel were familiar territory to her and well within the capabilities of one who often undertook longer and more hazardous voyages. This, however, was a daunting enterprise when one considers the risks involved to Grace herself. Very few Irish chieftains would, at this time, have dared to put foot on English soil, especially if a record of their anti-government activities had preceded them there. Grace must have had great confidence in her powers of persuasion, that her case would firstly be entertained, that an actual audience with the Queen would be granted and that she would not be hanged as a pirate and a rebel. It is true that she did have some influence at court in the person of Thomas, Duke of Ormond, known as Black Tom, who was emerging as one of Elizabeth's favourites, and whom Grace had obliged on occasion in the shipment of illegal cargo. The risks involved from the actual voyage were also great. Rumours of an imminent Spanish invasion were rife and the seas about the southern coasts of Ireland and England were constantly patrolled by English warships. The capture of an Irish ship captained by a notorious pirate would have been no mean prize for any privateer.

Nothing daunted, her ship crept around the south coast, past the Old Head of Kinsale and then keeping further out to sea, across the channel, past Lands End and the Isles of Scilly, through the Straits of Dover, and finally into the narrow estuary of the Thames, where the small ship must have been dwarfed by the soaring masts of English shipping. What were Grace's reactions to this city, the then hub of the universe? The hustle and bustle of London with its narrow coblestoned streets and alleys, its extremes of poverty and riches, its colour and pageantry, its milling crowds and loud noises, a city alive and vital, the centre of administration, power and trade. Grace must have pondered how her life, so removed from what she was now experiencing, could be controlled and administered by the powers of this strange world?

How London, and especially the court of Elizabeth, reacted to Grace and her followers has not been documented. Legend would lead us to believe that dressed in her Irish costume and barefoot the court of Elizabeth stared in disbelief at the strange apparition. This may or may not be true. As the wife of The MacWilliam she had attended social gatherings in the governor's residence in Galway and by Lord Deputy Sidney's own account she would seem to have made a pleasing appearance. In this, the climax of her social career, there seems little doubt but that Grace would have dressed as befitted the occasion.

London Bridge as Grace would have seen it. By Visscher, 1616. (National Library of Ireland)

Manuscript facsimile of Grace O'Malley's petition to Queen Elizabeth I in 1593

To be answered by Grany Himaly

201
62

1 Who was her ffather and mother?

2 Who was her first husband

3 What children she had by him, what be their names and where they are

4 What countries they have to maintaine them withall

5 To whom they be marryed

6 What ... her first husband & Sir m Hedough, if it stirreth at the court

7 To answer the like questions for her 2 husband and for his ... and their lyvings

8 If she were to be allowed her dower, or 3 of her husband being of what ... the same might be of

9 Whether upon the composition of Connaugh she hath been any petitioner for the wynd

10 Whether it be not against the custom of Ireland for the wyfe to have any ... after the decease of their husband then they brought with them

11 How she hath mayntenanc ... lyving since her last husband's death

12 Of what ... is Walter Bourgh fitz Theobald, and Shane Bourgh ... Meyler & his ...

13 What disputes and countries lyes next to her first husband's possessions?

14 How doth possible the house of Morrishe upon ... the ... in Owen O'maly

15 What lands doth m Gibbon possess in ... country

16 Who doth possess the country named Carramore, and Mayn Cornell

202

Manuscript facsimile of the 18 Articles of Interrogatory addressed to 'Granny Himaly'

Manuscript facsimile of Grace's replies, with Burghley's observations in the margin

Sir William Cecil, 1st Baron Burghley, the Queen's Private Secretary in 1593

In the meantime in Connaught, Bingham had received
the news of Grace's departure for London. He realised
that she would not let such an opportunity pass without
enlightening Her Majesty and Burghley of conditions in
Connaught and giving full vent to her version of the in-
justices of his administration there. Conscious of the
difficulties he had encountered from the government
when the Burkes had filed their Book of Complaints
against him, Bingham sought to counteract immediately
what Grace might have to report. He dispatched the
following letter to Burghley:

> 'There be 2 notable traitours gon over, Sir Morrow
> Ne doe and Grainy O'Maly both rebelle from their
> childhoode and continually in accion; and if such be
> heard to complaine against the officer or rewarded
> with anything from her Majesties yt wilbe the
> highway to make more rebelles: but they may
> challenge their reward to be brydewell (prison), for
> notwithstanding that they have many pardons,
> there ys matter ynough of late found out against
> them to hang them by justice. Grany O'Maly is
> mother-in-law to the notable tratoure, the Devilles
> Hooke. Howbeit (my most honourable good Lord)
> let them directly accuse me of anything, and if I
> discharge not myself honestly I am to be punished
> for it: but if they be drawn on to make generall
> exclamations against me I do not doubt but your
> Honour will most Honourably and indifferently
> consyder of it, for if they bely (belie) me not, I care
> not what all of them say against me'.[4]

One can have some sympathy for Bingham in this his last
ditch effort to counteract the claims he knows will be
made by Grace and Sir Murrough-Ne-Doe against him in
London. His own personality deterred him from making
life easier, both for the Gaelic chiefs and for himself, by
the methods he adopted in implementing the Queen's

policies in Connaught. Few of the Connaught chieftains, Grace included, resisted the implementation of English law, but the methods Bingham employed they could not bear and consequently frequently rebelled. While later he states that although

> some in Court hath commended her for doing her Matie. good service but in hope of her amendment hereafter I forbeare to write any more of her Accions now assuringe myself if she contynew never so ill mynded she shall not be lyable to do much for how great soever any may make her which knoweth her not, I will never aske but a boat of XXX tonnes to beate her and all the boates and Galeyes belonging to the county of Mayo and (with god's assistance) dryve her and all their fleet into the sea.

GRACE AND ELIZABETH

Bingham's observations did not adversely affect her chances of securing an audience with the Queen, for at the beginning of September 1593 Grace received her summons to appear before Elizabeth, at Greenwich Castle. This castle was a favourite place of abode particularly during the summer months. 'The palace in Elizabeth's reign was a long irregular building, standing close to the river bank, to which all her Tudor predecessors had made rather random additions as more accommodation was required. Elizabeth's own desire for expansion was economically achieved by expelling in 1559 the Observant friars from their building, which adjoined the palace, and using it to house her retinue. The long elevation to the river was punctuated by towers, the largest of which projected forward so that its foundations were washed by the river at high tide. The whole structure was crowned with battlements, but the necessity for these defensive features was belied by the wide transomed windows, which looked northward up and down the broad curve of the river as it wound past the shore of the Isle of Dogs'[5]

The details of the meeting of these two women, each outstanding and unique in her own special role as ruler and leader and alike in their personal characteristics, must unfortunately remain in the realm of fantasy and legend. Curiosity must have been a motivation for them both, curiosity about each other. Elizabeth, as a ruler in a male-dominated preserve, must have marvelled at how Grace, without the supporting facilities of state that she herself enjoyed, could successfully lead and govern so effectively and perform all the exploits for forty years credited to her by Elizabeth's own Irish deputies and governors. Grace in turn must have been anxious to see this paragon of English power whose orders and plans had affected and altered her very lifestyle so completely. The palace of Elizabeth was far removed from the stone castles of the west of Ireland, fortresses which were built with comfort as the minimum and security the maximum consideration; whose bare walls were constantly exposed to the Atlantic; the luxury of the Elizabethan court must have been over-powering. We can picture the stately Tudor court of the Virgin Queen with its luxury, colour, culture and refinements. Tapestry-covered walls, carved oak wainscots and furniture, ceilings ornate with intricate plaster-work; the long corridors leading to the royal apartments humming with the subdued and modulated tones of courtiers, emissaries, petitioners and many fair and fragile court ladies in exquisite dress and shining jewels, powdered and coiffed like tropical birds, flitting hither and thither trading the latest court gossip. And among this gathering, Grace O'Malley, leader of men, seawoman without equal, pirate, trader, self-appointed ruler contrary to law and tradition but too powerful to be dethroned, an elderly woman whose lined and weather-beaten face proclaimed the harsh conditions of her trade.

Grace and Queen Elizabeth. Frontispiece to *Anthologia Hibernica*, Vol II, 1793

> Restless and dark, its sharp and rapid look
> Show'd a fierce spirit, prone a wrong to feel
> And quicker to revenge it. As a book
> That sunburnt brow did fearless thoughts reveal,
> And in her girdle was a skeyne of steel.[6]

Elizabeth and her court possibly did stare at the only Gaelic woman ever to appear at court.

> In the wild grandeur of her mien erect and high
> Before the English Queen she dauntless stood
> And none her bearing there could scorn as rude
> She seemed well used to power, as one that hath
> Dominion over men of savage mood
> And dared the tempest in its midnight wrath
> And thro' opposing billows cleft her fearless path.[7]

According to tradition Grace wore a chieftain's cloak of green over a yellow bodice and petticoat. A long mantle is said to have covered her head and body, while her hair was gathered on her crown and fastened with a silver bodkin. It is more likely, however, that Grace was dressed in the traditional dress of women of the higher ranks of Gaelic society. This would have consisted of a long linen saffron smock or *léine,* reaching to the ankles with long wide sleeves, under a long dress with the sleeves slit and tapered to allow the wide sleeves of the *léine* to hang through and with a low-cut bodice laced in front. Over this she would have worn the Irish *brat* or cloak, a large woollen, sleeveless cloak reaching to the ground with a fringe of fine wool all around and, at the neck, a deeper fringe to give the appearance of a fur-like collar. Shoes were in general use by all classes in Ireland, so the legend that Grace O'Malley went barefoot for her audience with Elizabeth is rather absurd. What a contrast in style the meeting of these two women produced — the sober dress of Grace and the elaborate and ornamental style of Elizabeth who despite her age had not lost her passion for

Grace O'Malley before the English Court. From an eighteenth century woodcut.

dress and jewellery. 'The Queen's dresses were not distinguished by refinement of taste: it was rather at a magnificent display that she aimed, and her predilection was for gowns richly embroidered and sewn with jewels, so that they were as encrusted with ornament as the buildings of the early English Renaissance. This passion became no less as she grew older, and at her death her wardrobe is said to have contained more than two thousand gowns, with all things answerable'.

Tradition states that at the introduction of these two remarkable women, Elizabeth held her hand high, but Grace was the taller of the two and the English queen had to raise her hand to that of the Irish woman. A portrait of the meeting is from an old engraving made two centuries later and professes to show the dress and attitude of Grace on that occasion. It is said that during her conversation with Elizabeth, which was conducted in Latin, one of the ladies-in-waiting perceived that Grace required a handkerchief. A minute cambric and lace one was handed to her. After using it she threw it into the fire but Elizabeth informed her that it was meant to be put in her pocket. Amazed, Grace declared that in her country they had a higher standard of cleanliness than to pocket a soiled article.

Elizabeth was in her declining years yet the chalk-like features, piercing eyes and haughty demeanour had made many, more powerful figures tremble; yet Grace, knowing her own long record of unloyal activities had preceded her to Elizabeth's court, dared to ask not necessarily for forgiveness but for special favours and protection from Elizabeth's own administrators in Ireland. Legend would have us to believe that the meeting of these two women was, from Grace's viewpoint, the meeting of equals; Grace in her capacity as queen of Connaught and Elizabeth in her capacity as queen of England, and that when Elizabeth offered to confer the title of 'Countess' on her, Grace haughtily declined on the basis that a title could not be conferred on one of equal rank. The character and intellect of Grace makes this legendary assertion absurd; Grace was a realist and a leader who fully realised the personal risk she undertook in her mission to Elizabeth and knew that she must tread warily indeed in presenting her case to the power in whose hands her very life rested.

Elizabeth's own correspondence after the meeting is in itself conclusive proof of how well Grace succeeded in her mission. Elizabeth had previously ordered Bingham to supply her with the background information regarding Grace's petition requests and she had also instructed him to advise her how best she could alleviate Grace's personal plight in Connaught. Bingham, sounding very doubtful about these special arrangements for this 'notable traitoress', states in his dispatch

> how her Matie: might consider Grany O Maly with somewhat out of her former lyvings I knowe not unles it be by allowing her the thirds of both the lyvings which her sayd husbands lefte their sonnes and I have never harde her complayne of either of them or do I think they will see her want themselves having it. What course your honour shall please I shall holde towards her and the rest I am in all duty most willing to performe the same having many tymes tryed to reclame them by lenity and faire meanes and when they conforme themselves and begin once to live quietly as becomith Subjects I never restrayne them of any lawfull and convenient favoure being most desirous of peace and some quiet dayes .[8]

The favours won by Grace from Elizabeth reflected on the one hand the courage and ability of Grace and on the other the admiration and compassion Elizabeth entertained for Grace. Shortly after the meeting, on 6th September 1593, the Queen wrote the following letter to Sir Richard Bingham:

'Where our Treazurer of England, by his letters in
July last, did inform you of the being here of three
several persons of that our Province of Connaught
under your charge, that is, of Sir Morogh O'Flaherty,
Knight, Grany ne Maly and Roobuck French,
requiring to understand your opinion of every of
them concerning their suits; we perceive by your late
letters of answer what your opinion is of them, and
their causes of complaint or of suit, whereof you have
given them no just cause. But where Grany ne Maly
hath made humble suit to us for our favour towards
her sons, Morogh O'Flaherty and Tibbott Burk, and
to her brother Donell O'Piper (na Piopa), that they
might be at liberty, we perceive by your letters that
her eldest son, Morogh O'Flaherty, is no trouble but
is a principal man of his country, and as a dutiful
subject hath served us when his mother, being then
accompanied with a number of disorderly persons,
did with her 'gallyes' spoil him; and therefore by
you favoured, and so we wish you to continue. But
the second son, Tibbott Burk, one that hath been
brought up civilly with your brother and can speak
English, is by you justly detained because he hath
been accused to have written a letter to Bryan
O'Rork, the late traitor's son, though it cannot be
fully proved but is by him utterly denied; and for
her brother Donald, he hath been imprisoned 7
months past, being charged to have been in company
of certain that killed some soldiers in a ward. But
for those two you think they may be both dismissed
upon bonds for their good behaviour, wherewith we
are content, so as the old woman may understand we
yield thereto in regard of her humble suit; so she is
hereof informed and departeth with great thankful-
ness and with many more earnest promises that she
will, as long as she lives continue a dutiful subject,
yea, and will employ all her power to offend and

prosecute any offender against us. And further, for the pity to be had of this aged woman, having not by the custom of the Irish any title to any livelihood or position or portion of her two husband's lands, now being a widow; and yet her sons enjoying their father's lands, we require you to deal with her sons in our name to yield to her some maintainance for her living the rest of her old years, which you may with persuasion assure them that we shall theirin allow of them; and you also shall with your favour in all their good causes protect them to live in peace to enjoy their livelihoods. And this we do write in her favour as she showeth herself dutiful, although she hath in former times lived out of order, as being charged by our Treasurer with the evil usage of her son that served us dutifully. She hath confessed the same with assured promises by oath to continue most dutiful, with offer, after her aforesaid manner, that she will fight in our quarrel with all the world'.[9]

The contents of the Queen's letter indicate that Grace was in fact granted all her requests by the Queen in spite of the opinions and recommendations of her governor, Bingham. Grace's son, although strongly suspected of collusion with O'Rourke, was to be freed, as was her brother Donal. The compassion shown by Elizabeth for Grace's personal plight is evidenced by the provision for her maintenance for the remainder of her life from her sons' estates and that the amount be deductible from their taxes payable to the state. It was an unprecedented act of clemency and understanding of a woman's plight on Elizabeth's part and Grace must have departed from the royal presence with her 'burden' much lightened.

Grace returned to Ireland and reached Mayo about 19th September. Her visit to the English court must have been the subject of much discussion and no doubt her lonely fortress of Rockfleet hummed as she told and re-told the

details of her exciting adventure. But the actual results of
her mission took longer to emerge. Bingham proved reluc-
tant to implement the Queen's commands regarding
Grace's welfare and the welfare of her son and brother, but
Grace was not prepared, after her hazardous endeavours,
to allow the provisions of the Queen's letter to be negated
by deliberate inaction. She sought to force and threaten
Bingham to implement the Queen's instructions. Finally,
Bingham acquiesced and on 24th November he wrote to
Lord Burghley: 'I have enlarged Grany O'Mally, her son
Tibbot and brother Donell na Pipee, upon such slender
surtyes (surities) as they gave us, the woman urging it some
importunely swering that she would elles repair presently
to England.[10]

The Queen, in providing for Grace and her family, had
neglected to obtain the sureties or pledges usually
extracted from a petitioner in lieu of favours to be conferred. Elizabeth had underestimated the capabilities
of the 'aged woman' who had appeared before her. The
apparent frailty and agedness belied the true extent of her
boundless energy and plotting talents. Bingham realised
that the Queen had, in effect, given Grace a carte blanche
to operate as she pleased and to return to her old trade of
'maintainance by land and sea', despite all Bingham's
past endeavours to render her powerless. If the provisions
of the Queen's letter were enacted, Grace could once more
put to sea in her galleys under the guise of fighting the
Queen's 'quarrel with all the world'. The consequences
of Grace's actions would have to be borne by Bingham
and these could be far-reaching indeed, as Bingham fully
realised, Grace's status as a leader had, since her successful
mission to London, risen to at least its former strength.
However, the Queen commanded and Bingham, with
pressure and threats from Grace, had to obey. Tibbot
was released from prison and pardoned, as was Donal who
faded into obscurity after this event. On his release,
Tibbot must have gone into action quickly on the English

side against his fellow-clansmen judging by Sir Ralph
Lane's dispatch to Burghley written on 4th January
1594: 'The late service done in Connought upon the relics
of the Devil's Hook, by young Tybalte Bourke, the son of
Granee O'Maillie, by the Governor lately set at liberty,
by virtue of Her Majesty's letters to him in that behalf
written, and brought unto Sir Richard by his mother
Grana. He hath by this means put in a good perpetual
pledge for his loyalty during his life.'[11]   This action by
Tibbot was the tentative start of what was to be a stormy
and uneasy alliance with the English authorities. Bingham,
while obeying the Queen's command regarding Tibbot
and Donal, took his own revenge by interpreting the
Queen's command in regard to Grace's own welfare in his
own fashion.

GRACE AND THE EARL OF ORMOND

On her return from the meeting with Elizabeth, Grace
resolved to combine her promises of loyalty to Elizabeth
with an effort to recoup her substantial losses. She
gathered together the remnants of her fleet and
strengthened it by acquiring additional galleys. Bingham
noted her movements with apprehension. He realised
that she was about to launch on a new chapter of her
career on sea, this time in the guise of fighting the Queen's
enemies. To thwart her ambitions, Bingham, contrary
to the laws of the Composition, cessed or quartered a
number of soldiers on her and her followers which
rendered her powerless and penniless. Bingham further
ordered Captain Strittas and a company of soldiers to
accompany her on all her sea voyages. The surveillance of
her activities plus the added hardships imposed on her
slender resources, by the quartering of soldiers on her
territory, was too great a strain so that finally, in late
1594 or early 1595, she was compelled to flee into
Munster to seek assistance from her old acquaintance
Thomas, Earl of Ormond.

Grace in the knowledge that Ormond's word carried some weight at the English court, requested his services to prepare and dispatch a petition on her behalf to the Lord Treasurer. On 17th April 1595 Ormond wrote: 'My very good Lord the bearer hereof Grany ni Maly has been so importunate upon me for my letter to you in her behalf as I could not refrain to write these few lines unto your Lordship by her — Though I was very loath considering your Lords weighty causes to trouble you with her private suite, declaration whereof I refer herself and so commiting her causes to your Lords good consideration I leave you to the blessed guidance of God. From Carrick. 17 April 1595, Yours to command. Thomas Ormond'.[12] From the tones of Ormond's letter it would appear that Grace was preparing for another visit to the English court. There is no record to show that she did undertake a second mission, however, so one must assume that her following petition was dispatched to the Treasurer. The petition reads:

> May it please your honourable good Lordship, Grany Ni Mally of Connaght in her Majesties Realm of Ireland widowe, whereas accordinge her earnest promes made in September 1593, she beinge then at Court to continue a dutiful subject to the quenes most excellent Majestie, sethens which time she procured all her sons, cusons, and followers of the Mailles with a number of gallies whereof some were built after her last return into Ireland furnished with men and victwelles at their own chardges, accompanied with a Capten Strittes and his band of souldiers to repaire to the sease, where in certain Illandes eighteen of the chieftest of the Burkes here under named, being proclaimed traitors and a great number of souldiors came to that place of the country where the supplant, her sonnes cusens and followers dwelled and then did place and cess themselves taking up meat and drinke after their own

serving and six pens per diem for every souldier and
four pens per diem for his mann, where they do
remain all these seavenn monethes without any cause
of service in that part of the country to be don. But
if privat respect impoverished the poore enhabitantes;
wasted the contrey disabled them to serve her
Majestie, deminished her heighnesses rentes and
enforced your suppliant and the rest beinge not
hable to sustain the butthann (burden) of that cesse
and to pay the said rent, to abandon and leave the
contrey and to withdrawe themselves into the
province of Monnster, where they do remain in great
distresses; which cesse is contrarie to the
couvenauntes promised on her Majesties behalf in
discharge whereof your suppliant and the rest with all
the inhabitants of Connaght have yielded to pay
unto her highness that yearlie rent by the name of
comossission (Composition) rent. In regard of all
which and that your suppliant, her sonnes cusens
and followers will serve with a hundred menn at their
own chardges at sease uponn the coaste of Ireland in
her Majesties warres upon all occasions every yeare
for eister (Easter) till Mighelmas (Michaelmas), and
hafter to continue dutifull unto her Majestie, as true
and faythful subjectes ought to do; most humbly do
I beseech your Honourable Lordship, to be a means
to the Queenes most excellent Majestie to accept a
surrender of your suppliants sonnes and cusens, of
all their maners, castles, Illandes, townes, lands and
herediturents in Connaught aforesaid to be
immediately holden from her Majestie her heirs and
successors, in maner and formm, as in the schedoll
hereunto anexed is set downn, and to that effect to
grant her gratous letters to the Lord deputie of
Ireland uppon the acceptance of the said surrenders
to passe the same over to you suppliantes sons cusens
and followers may be suffered to inhabit and dwell

upon their ancient patrimony and inheritance paing the said rentes and other duties comprised in the indentors past and confermed in her Majesties behalf and all the lordes, cheftains, gentlemen friholders of Connaight aforesaid and your supliant, her sons and the rest will not only put their lives at all tymes in daunger to the advancement of her heighness service but also pray for your honourable lordships' successe long to lyve in happiness .[13]

Grace's plight was desperate. Bingham would give her no respite despite the explicit provisions made for her in the Queen's letter. He realised her potential for intrigue and rebellion much better than Elizabeth. The situation was highly charged in the north where O'Neill and O'Donnell were building up their forces for the great offensive and Connaught was waiting for the call to arms. Bingham realised that Grace's abilities, especially on the seas, would be eagerly engaged by her friends O'Donnell and O'Neill for the transport of men and arms to the battle areas or into Connaught to raise the rebellion. He was determined that this situation would not develop.

There is no record of any reply from the Treasurer or the privy council to the petition and later, on 5 May 1595, Grace petitioned Burghley again in the same vein: 'For her Majesty's letters to the Lord Deputy to put her in quiet possession of the third parts of the lands of her late husbands M'William and O'Flaherty and to live secure of her life'.[14] This is the final recorded petition by Grace, the final attempt to secure what, in her opinion, had been wrongfully withheld from her. It would seem that it was not only the English administration in Connaught but her own sons, especially Murrough in Bunowen, who had treated her unjustly in her declining years by withholding from her the third of their estates which she deemed was hers by right. However, it would seem also that Grace had forfeited her right to any inheritance, especially from the

O'Flaherty estates, when she abandoned her first husband's territory in order to obtain power and fortune as a leader in her own right in Mayo. Her marriage to Richard-an-Iarainn further nullified her claim to any part of the O'Flaherty possessions. Now at sixty-five years of age, she was still faced with the problem of securing her own survival. With the worsening situation in Ulster and Connaught, her latest petitions would seem to have received little attention.

O'DONNELL IN CONNAUGHT

In June 1595, the castle of Sligo, which was regarded as the key to the defence of Connaught against invasions by O'Donnell from the north, was held by George Bingham aided by Ulick Burke of Clanrickard. Ulick Burke and his followers mutinied, killed George Bingham and turned the castle over to O'Donnell. O'Donnell had now free access to Connaught. As he marched into Mayo the Burkes, including Grace and Tibbot-ne-Long, flocked to his side. Richard Bingham who was in Dublin hurried westwards but O'Donnell, not willing to give battle yet, slipped back to Sligo castle where Bingham owing to the usual lack of men and supplies was unable to besiege him. Meanwhile, O'Neill, anxious for time to regroup and prepare for his all-out offensive, made overtures of peace to the Queen. Elizabeth, eager to end the costly and indecisive war, ordered her generals to desist from offensive operations against O'Neill and O'Donnell and a truce was made in October to last until January.

At this time, Mayo, Sligo, Leitrim and north Roscommon were in the hands of O'Donnell and his supporters, and petty warfare among rival factions had commenced again. A new conspiracy for the removal of Bingham from the office of governor of Connaught was afoot, led by his adversaries, Theobald Dillon, Anthony Brabazon, Justice Dillon and other commissioners. Allegations, some of them quite unfounded, were lodged against

him and he was ordered for trial in Athlone to give
account of his services and practices during his governor-
ship of Connaught. Fearing that the trial was fixed against
him, Bingham fled to England where he was promptly
imprisoned. Sir Conyers Clifford was appointed governor
in his place.

Mayo was unified in its support of O'Donnell, and with
Bingham's departure the support grew daily. O'Donnell
arrived at Kilmaine in December 1595 and decided to
re-establish the MacWilliam title which had been abolished
by Bingham. A new MacWilliam was to be installed. The
contenders for the title were the senior Burke, William of
Shrule; Edmund of Cong; John, son of Richard, son of
John of the Termon; Richard, son of the Devil's Hook;
David and Oliver, sons of Sir John, Theobald, son of
Walter Kittagh and Grace's son, Tibbot-ne-Long. All the
chiefs of Mayo, among them The O'Malley, MacJordan,
MacCostello, MacMaurice, O'Dowd, the chiefs of the
various septs of the Mayo Burkes and Grace were present
at this gathering from which would emerge the new
MacWilliam and chief of the Mayo Burkes. With her old
friend O'Donnell assuming the role of inaugurator, Grace's
hopes were high that Tibbot-ne-Long might yet assume the
title previously held by his father. But this was not to be.
O'Donnell conferred the title on Theobald, son of Walter
Kittagh, who had been active in O'Donnell's cause. 'The
appointment was an unwise act, which weakened
O'Donnell's influence in Mayo by giving offence to every
family of the Burkes, whose rights and feelings were
openly disregarded'.[15]   It was a devastating setback for
Grace. With the departure of Bingham and the decline of
English power in the province and with Mayo in
O'Donnell's hands her hopes for an improvement in her
own and her son's political status had been rekindled. In
return for her frienship and previous co-operation with
O'Donnell, she had reason to expect his support for her
son's political aspirations. But O'Donnell decided other-

wise and in so doing alienated Tibbot-ne-Long from his cause. It was a mistake O'Donnell was to regret.

Thomas (Black Tom), Earl of Ormond

Chapter VII

THE END OF AN ERA

TIBBOT NE LONG

Elizabeth's war with The O'Neill and O'Donnell continued despite the truce. O'Donnell maintained and extended his hold over Connaught. His appointee to the MacWilliamship, Theobald MacWalter Burke, had not secured the loyalty of the other septs of the clan, who had in the first instance strongly disputed the appointment. Theobald continued as The MacWilliam only so long as O'Donnell was willing and able to support him. With few exceptions, notably the disgruntled septs of the Burkes, all the important chiefs and clans of Mayo rallied to O'Donnell's cause. In the north, O'Neill continued his show of loyalty to the Queen who had no option but to believe him; a method of bringing her one-time protégé 'him whom she had raised from the dust', to his knees appeared nowhere in sight.

Sir Conyers Clifford, who succeeded Bingham as governor of Connaught, took up the position during January 1597. O'Donnell's many incursions into Connaught via Ballyshannon resulted in the devastation of the countryside and Clifford reported that famine-like conditions existed in the province and that he had great difficulty in feeding his troops. Clifford toured his province during February and dispersed his army of 1,400 men to guard various English strongholds throughout Connaught. Sligo castle was recovered and garrisoned by him, aided by O'Connor of Sligo. In Mayo, The MacWilliam, unable to muster any strength, now that his protector O'Donnell was back in Ulster, was driven out. At Lahinch, in April 1596, Tibbot-ne-Long, Richard the son of the Devil's Hook and other Mayo chieftains, offered for terms and threw in their lot to fight with the Queen's forces against O'Neill and O'Donnell.

Grace was sixty years old at this time and would seem to have settled permanently at Rockfleet. Her son's decision to fight with the English against her former ally, O'Donnell, no doubt received her approval, as once again survival was at stake and the English this time offered the best terms for the procurement of that basic and prized commodity. Her disappointment at O'Donnell's decision regarding the MacWilliam title must have been surpassed only by her son's. Furthermore, her country had been ravaged and wasted repeatedly by O'Donnell and his MacWilliam in their search for cattle and booty to sustain their troops.

Grace's galleys, now that Bingham had departed, were able to put to sea more often in search of maintenance and her ships were reported to be operating off the coast of Thomond, where the Earl was obliged to do battle with some of her followers who had come ashore in search of plunder. It was a grim time along the west coast with the land bare of cattle and produce and clan after clan divided in their loyalties, some fighting for the Queen's cause, others with O'Neill and O'Donnell. It is unlikely that Grace brooded over her misfortune but rather set about resolving it, and with her son away on his warring missions, her own ability and enterprise were her only refuge. One of her raiding excursions at this time was reported to the Council by the Dean of Limerick, who stated 'MacNeil of Barra and Grany ny Mallye invaded one another's possessions though far distant'.[1] Whether an attack or a reprisal this incident established that Grace continued to be active in her trade, a remarkable feat at her advanced age.

Tibbot-ne-Long, Richard Burke, son of the Devil's Hook, and the other chieftains who had decided to align with the English, met Clifford at Castlebar to submit and receive their pardons for past offences. They agreed to pay the arrears in the Composition rent and to give pledges for their good behaviour and loyal support. (This custom of 'giving pledges' was a widespread practice in sixteenth-century Ireland and meant that when a chief submitted and was pardoned he gave his son or relatives into the care of the English authorities, depending on the importance of his status as chieftain and the seriousness of his crimes. If he broke his promise of loyalty, his 'pledge' could be legally killed by the English as recompense for the chief's misconduct.) Clifford in turn secured their pardon and provided them with beef, a very scarce commodity at the time. The agreement was signed by Oliverus MacShane Burke, Oliverus MacEdmund, Tibbot Burke, Richard Burke, alias the Devil's Hook's son, David Burke, Owen O'Malley, Mac Jordan and others. According to H. T. Knox, 'these names are taken partly from an original at Westport House, which must have been a duplicate in possession of Tibbot-ne-Long, now not entirely legible, and partly from a copy in the Public Record Office in London'.[2] As a pledge for himself and his sept, Tibbot gave his son, Grace's grandson, Moylar or Myles Burke, to the English. Tibbot realised that he himself was a valuable asset to the English given his superior seamanship, his strength as a leader in Mayo, his sizeable fleet and his absolute knowledge of the entire coastline, accomplishments inherited from his remarkable mother. Beef and a pardon, however, were hardly a fair exchange for these valuable talents, so Tibbot presented Clifford with a list of demands which were dispatched to the English Privy Council for their consideration. On 25th June, an abstract of the demands and the Privy Council's decisions regarding them was recorded thus: 'An abstract of the Demands of Theobald ne Long Burke unto Sir Coniers Clifford, Governor of Connaught, at Lehinche 25 April 1597; sent unto England and answered by the Lords of the Council 25 June 1597'.[3] In it Tibbot asks for aid from her Majesty's forces to banish The MacWilliam and to secure his lands and a 'title according to the worthiness of his service'. Although this was granted to him, Tibbot was unable to banish The MacWilliam and he had to wait many years before a title was conferred on him. He asked that lands, unfairly seized in Sir Richard Bingham's time, be returned to their rightful owners; this was denied. He asked for 'Her Majesty's letters' on behalf of his step-brother, Murrough O'Flaherty of Bunowen, and on behalf of his mother and this request was granted. He asked that the Devil's Hook's son should be pardoned and have a pension and this was granted. Tibbot was also granted possession of all rebels' lands, rebels of his own sept. His demand for possession of the castle and lands of Castlebar was denied but he received a company of foot soldiers in the Queen's pay for his use. He also secured pardons for other relations. The fact that his demands were con-sidered by the Privy Council was proof enough that the English considered the procurement of his services a valuable asset. Tibbot had made a good bargain and if he happened to be on the winning side at the final outcome of the war, his future looked bright indeed.

Tibbot's bargain with the English must have secured greater freedom of movement for Grace and her galleys and it is likely that she took full advantage of the free rein. Tibbot was his mother's son; he had inherited Grace's intuition, wiliness and foresight, qualities which had sus-tained her throughout her life and had enabled her to out-manoeuvre anyone or anything English or Gael had put as an obstacle in her path to personal gain and achieve-ment. Tibbot, however, kept his bargain for the most part with the English and his name appears in many of the dispatches of the English generals and governors in the final years of the war with O'Neill and O'Donnell. Grace's other son, Murrough O'Flaherty, also sided with the English, as he had tended to do in the past, and both he and Tibbot were created captains of their own followers.

Grace backed her sons' decision to fight on the side of the English and she would seem to have profited also by her sons' agreements with Clifford, who stated in a dispatch to the Lord Deputy in August 1597 that he had 'given him (Tibbot), his *mother* and brother amongst them in money and other necessaries, £200'[4] for their valuable services by sea.

BATTLES OF THE YELLOW FORD
AND THE CURLEW MOUNTAINS

On 14 August 1598, the English were overwhelmed by the forces of O'Neill and O'Donnell at the Battle of the Yellow Ford. One thousand Connaughtmen in O'Donnell's pay fought in the battle. O'Donnell now had a free run of Connaught and raided deep into Thomond. In the autumn, O'Donnell sent his MacWilliam and O'Doherty into Murrisk and Burrishoole (i.e. Owle Uachtarach and Owle Iochtarach) with orders to seize all the cattle herds in the area. The deed is remembered in the lines of the poem:

> Grainne na gCearbhach do creach
> Is Clann Ghuibuin na ngreadh n-uaibhreach.

> Grace of the Gamblers be plundered
> And the Clan Gibbons of proud steeds.

With Tibbot and the other chieftains of the area away fighting in the war, Grace could offer little resistance to the intruders from the north and she watched helplessly, as the Annals of the Four Masters record: 'They collected all the cattle that were on the mainland outside the small islands, and though great was the gathering and collection of preys, they made, they encountered no danger or difficulty on account of them, save only the trouble of removing and driving them off'. These cattle raids were usually accompanied by the general plunder of property and countryside. Since the attack by Captain Martin in 1574 on Grace's fortress of Rockfleet, there is no indication that its stout defences came under attack again and Grace was left in relative safety inside its walls.

Tibbot, with his stepbrother, Murrough O'Flaherty, commanded three large galleys, each able to contain 300 men, off the west coast. In July 1599, Governor Clifford was ordered to transport supplies, military stores and building materials by sea to Sligo. Tibbot sailed with the cargo from Galway city and anchored off Sligo bay and waited for Clifford's arrival. A detachment of O'Donnell's troops kept him under constant surveillance. On 15th August Clifford attempted to cross the Curlew mountains. O'Donnell's men held the pass, attacked and routed the English, leaving Clifford among the dead. It was a resounding victory for O'Donnell and many of the Gaelic chiefs, who up to now had either fought with the English or had been undecided either way, submitted and joined his cause. Among them was O'Connor Sligo, Tibbot's brother-in-law. Tibbot still maintained his position off the coast and made no move to submit to O'Donnell who, the day after the battle, realising the importance to the campaign of Tibbot's services, attempted to induce him to join his cause. Tibbot sent Murrough O'Flaherty to parley with O'Donnell who suggested that Tibbot should serve the O'Donnell cause by seizing English shipping in the area. Perhaps O'Donnell's terms were not substantial enough, or perhaps with his inherited foresight Tibbot realised that, although O'Donnell was now at the height of his power, the day would finally be won by the English, and it was on the winning side Tibbot intended to be; for one reason or another, Tibbot slipped anchor and sailed with his cargo still intact back to Galway city. O'Donnell might well regret the alienation of Tibbot from his cause; the seamanship which Tibbot and his clan possessed were now vital to the outcome of the war, in the speedy transport of men and equipment from one place to another. The English had realised the real value of Tibbot's services and had offered him the best terms first.

The year 1600 saw the fortunes of O'Neill and
O'Donnell at their highest. O'Neill had brought the war
right into the heart of Munster, while O'Donnell had subdued Connaught. Elizabeth, in a final effort to secure her
now almost lost kingdom, sent Lord Mountjoy and Sir
George Carew against O'Neill and O'Donnell. The government realised the danger to England's security should
Ireland, in Gaelic hands, become the entry point for Spain
into England. O'Neill's dispatches to the Spanish court
made an invasion from Spain seem imminent. Sir Francis
Bacon had warned the parliament earlier 'that ulcer of
Ireland . . . hath run on and raged more, which cannot but
attract the ambition of Spain'.[5] In May 1600, Henry
Docwra landed behind O'Neill's defences on the Foyle
with 4,000 troops while Mountjoy and Carew attacked
Ulster and Munster, destroying everything in their path.

THE FINAL RECORD OF GRACE O'MALLEY

While Tibbot features in many of the English dispatches
of this time and his exploits during and after the war
against O'Neill and O'Donnell are well recorded, no
records of Grace's life and activities exist. Now some
seventy years old, Grace must have left her struggle both
with the world and the sea in her son's capable hands. The
final recorded reference to her name appears in the State
Papers for July 1601. It is a dispatch from one of the
Queen's naval captains, Captain Charles Plessington, who
was on patrol off the western sea coast on the look-out
for the daily expected Spanish invasion force, and is
written to the Queen's private secretary, Sir Robert Cecil.
In the dispatch Captain Plessington states:

> . . . I came hither, where I have spent two months in
> plying off and on at sea upon the west coasts of
> Ulster and Connaught, doing my beast endeavour to
> intercept and take any ship, bark, or other vessels
> from Spain or other parts, which shall bring relief

or give aid unto the rebels . . . Right Honourable, amongst all the most fair and goodly rivers and havens of this coast, I have found out the place where the Spaniards, at their first arrival, do harbour themselves, to learn news and take in pilots. This river is upon the westernmost part of Connaught, between Cape Achill and Cape Killala, whereof lies certain rocks called Stags, from which this river runs into the country of O'Burkes, due south and north. I know no name for it yet. But hither came two ships from Spain with treasure and munition at Christmas last. Here they stayed a fortnight and from whence they went to Teelin and Killibeggs, and there remained one month in discharging of their loding . . .

The captain's observations provide an insight into the activities of the people who occupied this remote coastal territory. Spanish vessels on their way to Ulster frequently used Clew bay, Blacksod bay, Achill sound and other inlets along the coastline as their first port of call, in order to secure information on the position of English patrol ships in the area, information on the war situation and especially to secure the services of able and trustworthy pilots who would steer them safely along the dangerous coast to Ulster. For a fee or for barter, these services were to be purchased from the O'Malleys, the Burkes and the O'Flaherties, the families who had provided this service down through the centuries. Though the two Spanish ships referred to by Plessington were quite obviously on their way north with military supplies for O'Neill and O'Donnell, this would not have deterred either Grace, the Burkes or the O'Malleys. The provision of pilots and information was a matter of business and where business was concerned, for Grace and her fellow Burkes and O'Malleys, it came first in their order of priority. Plessington continues with an interesting account of the opposition he encounters from one of Grace's galleys which was on its way to plunder McSweeney country in Donegal, until its interception by the English warship:

> All the sails I have seen since I came upon the coast was a galley I met withal betwixt Teelin and Killibeggs, where I made her run on shore amongst the rocks, notwithstanding she rowed with thirty oars, and had on board, ready to defend her, 100 good shot, which entertained skirmish with my boat at most an hour and had put her to the worst. But coming up with my ship to her rescue, I quickly with my great shot made an end to the fray. This galley comes out of Connaught, and belongs to Grany O'Malley, whereof a base son of hers is Captain, and, as I learned since, this with one other galley, was set out and manned with a people called the Flaherties, who was purposed to do some spoils upon the countries and islands of McSwyne Fanad and MacSwyne ne Doe, about Lough Swilly and Sheep haven. From on board Her Majesty's ship Tremontaney lying at sea off the Blackrock, 1601 July 17.[6]

That the captain of the galley was Grace's 'base son' is unlikely. The error in identification is thought to have arisen in the translation of the information, which would have been given by the crew of the galley in Irish to the English captain. That he was an O'Malley and possibly related to Grace is likely, as Grace's two sons were at that time employed elsewhere in the services of the English and there is no evidence to suggest that Grace had other sons. That Grace was alive at this time seems likely, and although unable through age to partake actively in maritime expeditions, it would appear that under her direction her trade of maintenance by land and sea was being continued by her followers.

Thus the extraordinary career of Grace O'Malley ends as it begins, shrouded in uncertainty. The exact date of her death, as of her birth, is uncertain. From the evidence to hand it would seem that her death occurred at Rockfleet, about the year 1603. She possibly did survive to hear of the defeat of her former friends, O'Neill and O'Donnell, at the battle of Kinsale, the final and conclusive milestone in Elizabeth's campaign to reconquer her Irish kingdom. The struggle had been long, arduous and expensive in both money and man-power; many of Elizabeth's most able generals and administrators died in the Irish campaign.

The old Gaelic order had maintained a resistance, albeit tattered, throughout the decades. But resistance, if it were to prove effective, depended on unified opposition and well-planned foreign aid, and neither of these materialised when most required. The old Gaelic order in the sixteenth century was geared to the system which provided for separate states and territories ruled by chieftains and lords, independent of each other yet depending on one another's strength. The survival of the fittest was manifest in the system's laws and regulations and therein lay its greatest weakness. Ireland had become detached from the mainstream of European political and social practices and was still, in the sixteenth century, a medieval state.

Grace had been born when Gaelic power was at its highest point in the century, and yet the very seeds for its destruction were being sown by Henry VIII. She had experienced the effects of English policies on her way of life and had at first actively resisted as did most of the Gaelic chieftains and lords of her time. She recognised sooner than most, however, the futility of unorganised resistance against the concentrated and effective methods of a unified and powerful enemy. English presence and eventual domination was, at the end of the day, the likely outcome. She realised that in order to survive the upheavals one had to adapt one's policies and position as the changing political climate demanded, and this she did effectively.

GRACE'S LEADERSHIP

In order to survive under either the old or the new system, a chieftain had to possess certain qualities of leadership. He had to be prepared to risk the same dangers as his followers and be able to command their respect and loyalty. Given the prevalence for changing allegiances during the sixteenth century, the task of controlling and retaining the loyalty of one's followers was a difficult task. Yet Grace, a woman in a man's world, possessed and retained the loyalty and obedience of her followers to the end of her lengthy career. Courage and the ability to succeed, coupled with a certain magnetism of personality, were the hall-marks of this remarkable leader of men. A domineering personality alone was not enough to spur men on to risk their lives in a perilous service led and controlled by a woman. But Grace was not content to direct her operations from the safety of the shore or from her stout fortresses. She braved the dangers with her followers and by her own courage ensured the courage and loyalty of her men. Her followers, moreover, were not all of her own clan, or even of the one clan, but were comprised of men from the O'Flaherty, O'Malley, Burke, O'Dowd, Conroy, MacNally and MacPhilbin clans, each with their inter-tribal feuds and grudges which had to be subdued and eliminated if Grace was to mould them into a force whose only loyalty would be to her alone.

This ability to command and to retain the respect and loyalty of her men is one of the outstanding features of Grace's character and given the century and the life-style is even more remarkable. Very few women in history have possessed this characteristic. One can point to Elizabeth's long rule over England during the same period, as a more powerful example. Yet Elizabeth inherited a well organised and long-established position and kingdom; Grace constructed her own 'kingdom' and installed herself as its leader, contrary to Gaelic and English laws alike.

Elizabeth had access to all the supporting facilities of state to make her task of governing less difficult; Grace ruled her 'kingdom' alone.

Grace's husbands, certainly Richard-an-Iarainn, were well mastered by her, as Lord Deputy Sidney confirms in his report when he states 'for she was as well by sea as by land, well more than Mrs. Mate with him'. Further evidence of her independence of and dominance over her husbands is demonstrated by the fact that she is always referred to in the State Papers and elsewhere as Grace O'Malley, never Grace O'Flaherty or Grace Burke. Sidney in reference to her first appearance before him in 1577 states, 'there came to me also a most famous feminine sea captain called Grany Imallye . . . she brought with her her husband . . .', leaving us in no doubt that Grace was the dominant partner in her marriage to Richard-an-Iarainn.

Courage and daring, however, were not enough to sustain loyalty if that loyalty was not rewarded. Grace had no option but to be successful on land and especially on sea, if she were to maintain credence as a leader. The fact that she was a woman made success even more necessary. Her career of trade and piracy was a success. Her trade was a difficult and uncertain occupation, given the conditions of the time and the prohibitive bye-laws concerning the use of Galway port; but she supplemented her income by engaging in the more lucrative but dangerous occupation of piracy, which was also a highly competitive business along the west coast. That she was successful in this is beyond doubt and the State Papers provide the evidence of the extent of her success. Galway was a thriving city at this time and the ships using the port facilities there, from which she was debarred, provided Grace with much of her 'maintainance'. Against her agile and speedy galleys, the lumbering merchant ships were easy prey and paid the penalty. On land Grace exacted similar penalties from inhabitants along the coast from

Kerry to Donegal.

Piracy was a widespread sixteenth-century occupation and was not regarded in such an unfavourable light as one might expect today. It had become a way of life for those connected with the sea, not only along the west coast of Ireland, but in England and on the Continent as well. The century produced many notable seamen whose main claim to fame, apart from some military exploits, was the fact that they were expert pirates whose ships seldom failed to sail into port laden with treasures and spoils of their piratical activities. There was little difference then, only in extent, between the activities of Drake and Raleigh along the Spanish coasts, and those of Grace O'Malley along the coasts of Ireland. It is ironic that although Drake and Raleigh are considered the fathers of the British navy, one of Ireland's few seafarers of note, Grace O'Malley, is not considered worthy of remembrance by Ireland's naval authorities. It is amazing to note that even the fishery protection vessel *Grainne* is named, not after Grace O'Malley, but after the legendary Grainne of Celtic mythology.

Grace also, as her ancestors had done, provided a service for the swift transport of men and supplies from one territory to another. The O'Neills and O'Donnells in Ulster particularly engaged her services frequently for the transport of mercenaries from Scotland. The employment of Scots mercenaries in the Burke rebellion in Mayo meant added business for Grace, as Perrott pointed out to the Queen when he wrote regarding the reasons for the kidnapping of Hugh Roe O'Donnell. Grace also provided a pilot service for foreign vessels, whose knowledge of the treacherous western coastline was negligible. She was also successful in her career on land and, by her own admission, had amassed a cattle and horse herd numbering 1,000 head.

She subdued much of Mayo and her name is associated with many castles in the west of Ireland such as Hen castle in Lough Corrib; Bawn castle and Castleleaffy near Westport; Kinturk castle near Castlebar and Renvyle castle (Currath castle) in Connemara, where her attack on its yielding defences are remembered in the lines of the poem:

No braver seaman took a deck in hurricane or squalls
Since Grace O'Malley battered down old Currath Castle's walls.

One of the earliest references to Grace recalls how she repulsed the attack of Captain Martin, his troops and ships on Rockfleet castle.

GRACE'S SEAMANSHIP

In order to accomplish even part of what she is accredited with in her career on the seas, Grace must have had expert knowledge of seamanship. Although imbued with a love for the sea life since childhood, it was no mean accomplishment on the part of a woman to have mastered and excelled in the skills of seamanship and survive to remember it in old age. To endure and survive the wild Atlantic along the dangerous western coast of Ireland was some feat. Coupled with this, her ability to navigate her ships on voyages to Ulster, Munster, Scotland, England and Spain must rank her with the best seamen of her time. Knowledge of navigation, sound judgement of the tides, currents, skies and winds; knowledge of the capabilities of the ships she sailed and a thorough knowledge of the dangerous coastline with its tricky currents, protruding headlands and hidden reefs, these were the basic requirements for survival at sea. The dangers to be encountered from English patrol ships out to capture her, or from competitors in the piracy trade out to relieve her of her cargo and possibly her life, made sea life in the sixteenth century along the Irish coasts, even more hazardous. Her love of the maritime way of life is neatly illustrated in a legend. She gave a seed to each of her three sons to plant. The first and second sons planted theirs in fertile soil and carefully tended them throughout the year until the stalks grew strong and tall. The third son, however, took his seed and threw it into the ocean. After some time Grace asked her three sons what they had done with the seeds. The first and second sons told how they had planted their seeds in fertile soil and had carefully tended them throughout the year. But the third son said 'I set mine in the deepest and most fertile soil of all — the ocean'. 'You are my son', said Grace.

GRACE'S POLITICAL STRATEGY

If one considers the political stand of Grace O'Malley without considering the era to which she belonged, then she must emerge at best an enigma or worst a traitor. Born into an ancient Gaelic family who had governed their territory according to the Brehon law and Gaelic custom, her father unlike his contemporaries, had never submitted to an English governor or Lord Deputy. Yet, his daughter sought and gained pardon from the English queen in order to secure her rights; she aligned herself at times with the forces whose ambitions were to destroy the Gaelic world into which she was born while, at the same time, aided those who were seeking to preserve it. When Grace's political involvement in the affairs of Connaught is placed within the context of the time, she emerges as a realist. Patriotism was not applicable to this sixteenth century Ireland. Survival was the spur either to resist the English if one was powerful enough or to accept the changes to whatever degree would guarantee survival. Ireland was still the nation of individual and divided loyalties, where Irish fought Irish and Irish and English combined against Irish in the continuous battle for personal advancement and power. In Grace's position, to hold on to what she had and to survive the political and social upheavals of the time was her only concern as it was the concern of every Gaelic chieftain and Anglo-Irish lord. The common enemy had not yet been identified and would not be until decades later, when the word patriotism might then be applied. Entrapped in the collision course of two widely differing systems, one had to be nimble of mind not to be trodden underneath in the scramble for political survival. Grace's political ability ensured her survival as a leader and power in Mayo for many years. She acknowledged English presence and power when, unrequested, she submitted to Lord Deputy Sidney in 1577. She played her part in securing the MacWilliam title for her undeserving husband, who had been too open in his hostilities towards the English. At the same time her standing in the Gaelic world did not diminish and, when the opportunity arose for supplementing her income, her services by sea were available to Gaelic and English alike. Under Bingham's administration in Connaught her fortunes and position underwent a complete reversal. Bingham was too shrewd an operator, too thorough an administrator to allow any transgression of the laws he was ordered to implement. Grace had transgressed too far and too often for his liking and he fully realised her capabilities and power and promptly set about stripping her of them. By appealing to Elizabeth over Bingham's head, Grace played her trump card. She bargained on Elizabeth's womanly instincts and sympathies and won the day. But it was Bingham, and not Elizabeth, who administered Connaught, dim and distant from the court in London, and while not directly opposing the Queen's wishes, Bingham managed to postpone her recommendations regarding Grace, indefinitely.

HER DESCENDANTS

From Grace's marriage to Richard-an-Iarainn sprang the Viscount Mayo line. Her son, Tibbot-ne-Long, was created first Viscount Mayo in 1627 by Charles I. This line became extinct in 1767. In 1669, her great-great-grand-daughter, Maud Burke, married John Browne of Westport and the present owner of Westport House, Lord Altamont, is the direct descendant of this couple. Portraits of Maud Burke and John Browne are on view in the great hall of Westport House today, the oldest portraits in the House's collection, while in the garden is a Mulberry tree planted during the couple's lifetime and still flourishing today. On the

Maud Burke (born c.1642), great great grand-daughter of Grace O'Malley, and wife of John Browne of Westport (Photograph by Liam Lyons of portrait in Westport House)

John Browne of Westport (Photograph by Liam Lyons from portrait in Westport House)

Below: Westport House, residence of Lord Altamont (Photograph by Liam Lyons)

O'Flaherty side, Grace's son, Murrough-na-Maor, and her grandson, Murrough-na-Mart (of the Beeves), continued to live at Bunowen castle but later, as English settlers and planters moved further westward, the O'Flaherties were dispossessed of their large domains. Some of her descendants emigrated and fought in foreign armies while others remained and clung grimly to the remnants of their heritage to die mainly in poverty.

HER IMPACT ON IRISH LITERATURE

Grace O'Malley's impact on Irish literature is an unusual one. While the factual evidence of her life has been ignored by Irish annalists and historians, Irish poets on the other hand have immortalised her memory by depicting her mainly as a symbolic and national figure. With the exception of a brief mention in the sixteenth-century poem addressed to Shane O'Doherty, the majority of the later poems depict Grace or Granuaile as symbolic of Ireland or in her own right as a figure of fiery patriotism. In the many national disturbances down through the centuries, when poems concerning the state of Ireland were outlawed, Grace O'Malley, along with Roisin Dubh and Caitleen Ni Houlihan, became one of the great poetic, nationalist symbols.

While Grace might indeed be amazed at her elevation to such an unusual pedestal, it is mainly through this rather strange literary anomaly that her memory survived the passing of time. During the nineteenth and twentieth centuries some fanciful and romantic novels, based loosely on her life, appeared. These were based mainly on the legends which had survived and had been magnified from century to century until the life of Grace O'Malley appeared to be too fantastic to be credible. While literature is to be commended for preserving her memory from complete oblivion, one must also fault it for preserving an image of her that bears little resemblance to her actual life. The English State Papers and manuscripts alone have preserved for posterity some facts about her character and career; from their records one can obtain a glimpse at least of Grace and her contribution to the affairs of the country during the traumatic age in which she lived.

A FORGOTTEN LADY

The life of Grace O'Malley ended as it began, at the edge of the ocean that had sustained her throughout her long and eventful life. History has yet to adequately acknowledge the role she played in the affairs of sixteenth-century Ireland. John O'Donovan, while writing for the Ordnance Survey of Mayo in 1838, states: 'She is now most vividly remembered by tradition, and people were living in the last generation who conversed with people that knew her personally. Charles Cormick of Erris, now 74 years and 6 weeks old, saw and conversed with Elizabeth O'Donnell of Newtown within the Mullet, who died about 65 years ago who had seen and intimately known a Mr. Walsh who remembered Grainne. Walsh died at the age of 107 and his father was the same age as Grainne'.[8] The Irish annalists, whether out of chagrin that a mere woman could figure so remarkably in the affairs of the time or because that era produced too many such remarkable personages or simply because of lack of space, completely excluded Grace from their records.

Today, Grace O'Malley tends to remain a figure of myth and legend, a fact that seems unjust to the memory of such a courageous woman. In the west of Ireland, her own stone fortresses alone stand in remembrance. Rockfleet castle, still intact, gloomily broods over the quiet waters of Clew bay, a solitary sentinel. Across the bay on Clare island, the ruins of 'Grania's castle' are still visible. The ruins of the Cistercian abbey on the island are said by some to contain the remains of Grace, while others avow that Burrishoole abbey is her final resting place. Through the neglect (and prejudice) of historians and annalists, most of her fascinating life remains a mystery and it is perhaps fitting that her final resting place should be hidden from the uncaring eyes of centuries which have neglected the reality of one of the most remarkable women in Irish history.

The O'Malley tomb at Clare Island Abbey where Grace O'Malley, according to tradition, is buried. See also photograph page 34 above. (Commissioners of Public Works).

GRANUAILE

There stands a tower by the Atlantic side
A grey old tower, by storm and sea-waves beat
Perch'd on a cliff, beneath it yawneth wide
A lofty cavern of yore a fit retreat
For pirates galleys; altho', now, you'll meet
Nought but the seal and wild gull; from that cave
A hundred steps do upwards lead your feet
Unto a lonely chamber! — Bold and brave
Is he who climbs that stair, all slippery from the wave.

I sat there on an evening. In the west,
Amid the waters, sank the setting sun:
While clouds, like parting friends, about him prest,
Clad in their fleecy garbs, of gold and dun;
And silence was around me — save the hum,
Of the lone and wild bee, or the curlew's cry.
And lo! upon me did a vision come,
Of her who built that tower, in days gone by;
And in that dream, behold! I saw a building high.

A stately hull — lofty and carved the roof —
Was deck'd with silken banners fair to see.
The hanging velvet, from Genou's woof,
And wrought with Tudor roses curiously;
At its far end did stand a canopy,
Shading a chair of state, on which was seen
A ladye fair, with look of majesty,
Amid a throng, 'yclad in costly sheen —
Nobles and gallant Knights proclaim her England's Queen.

The sage Elizabeth; and by her side
Were group'd her counsellors, with calm, grave air,
Burleigh and Walsingham, with others, tried
In wisdom and in war, and sparkling there,
Like Summer butterflies, were damsels fair,

Beautiful and young: behind a trusty band
Of stalwart yeomanry, with watchful care,
The portal guard, while nigher to it stand
Usher and page, ready to ape with willing hand.

A Tucket sounds, and lo! there enters now
A strange group, in saffron tunics drest:
A female at their head, whose step and brow
Herald her rank, and, calm and self possest,
Onward she came, alone through England's best,
With careless look, and bearing free yet high,
Tho' gentle dames their titterings scarce represt,
Noting her garments as she passed them by;
None laughed again who met that stern and flashing eye.

Restless and dark, its sharp and rapid look
Show'd a fierce spirit, prone a wrong to feel,
And quicker to revenge it. As a book,
That sun-burnt brow did fearless thoughts reveal;
And in her girdle was a skeyne of steel;
Her crimson mantle, a gold brooch did bind;
Her flowing garments reached unto her heel;
Her hair-part fell in tresses unconfined,
And part, a silver bodkin did fasten up behind.

'Twas not her garb that caught the gazer's eye —
Tho' strange, 'twas rich, and, after its fashion, good —
But the wild grandeur of her mien-erect and high.
Before the English Queen she dauntless stood,
And none her bearing there could scorn as rude;
She seemed as one well used to power — one that hath
Dominion over men of savage mood,
And dared the tempest in its midnight wrath,
And thro' opposing billows cleft her fearless path.

And courteous greeting Elizabeth then pays,
And bids her welcome to her English land

And humble hall. Each looked with curious gaze
Upon the other's face, and felt they stand
Before a spirit like their own. Her hand
The stranger raised — and pointing where all pale,
Thro' the high casement, came the sunlight bland,
Gilding the scene and group with rich avail;
Thus, to the English Sov'reign, spoke proud "Grana Wale".

Queen of the Saxons! from the distant west
I come; from Achill steep and Island Clare,
Where the wild eagle builds 'mid clouds, his nest,
And Ocean flings its billows in the air.
I come to greet you in your dwelling fair.
Led by your fame — lone sitting in my cave.
In sea — beat Doona — it hath reached me there,
Theme of the minstrel's song; and then I gave
My galley to the wind, and crossed the dark green wave.

"Health to thee, ladye! — let your answer be
Health to our Irish land; for evil men
Do vex her sorely, and have buklar'd thee
Abettor of their deeds; lyeing train,
That cheat their mistress for the love of gain,
And wrong their trust-aught else I little reck,
Alike to me, the mountain and the glen —
The castle's rampart or the galley's deck;
But thou my country spare — your foot is on her neck.

Thus brief and bold, outspake that ladye stern,
And all stood silent thro' that crowded hall;
While proudly glared each proud and manly kern
Attendant on their mistress. Then courtly all
Elizabeth replies, and soothing fall
Her words, and pleasing to the Irish ear —
Fair promises — that she would soon recall
Her evil servants. Were these words sincere?
That promise kept? Let Erin answer with a tear!

O'Hart, Vol. II, p.675 *Irish Pedigrees* (From the Irish)

GRANA WEAL

O thou that are sprung from the flow'r of the land,
Whose virtues endear and whose talents command;
When our foemen are banished, how then wilt thou feel
That the King of the right shall espouse Grana Weal.

O'er the high hills of Erin what bonfires shall blaze,
What libations be pour'd forth! — What festival days! —
What minstrels and monks with one heart-pulse of zeal,
Sing and pray for the King and his own Grana Weal!

The monarch of millions is riding the sea,
His revenge cannot sleep, and his guards will not flee;
No cloud shall the pride of our nobles conceal,
When the foes are dispersed that benight Grana Weal.

The mighty in thousands are pouring from Spain,
The Scots, the true Scots shall come back again;
To far distant exile no more shall they steal,
But waft the right King to his fond Grana Weal.

Raise your hearts and exult, my beloved at my words,
Your eyes to your King, and your hand to your swords! —
The Highlands shall send forth the bonnetted Gael,
To grace the glad nuptials of Grana Weal.

And Louis, and Charles and the heaven-guided Pope,
And the King of the Spaniards shall strengthen our hope;
One religion — one kindred — one soul shall they feel,
For our heart enthroned Exile and Grana Weal.

With weeping and wailing, and sorrow and shame —
And anguish of heart that no pity dare claim;
The craven English churls shall all powerless kneal
To the home-restored Stuart and Grana Weal.

Our halls will rejoice with friendship and cheer,
And our hearts be as free from reproach — as from fear;
The hungry adventurer shall pine for the meal,
He long lapped from the life-stream of Grana Weal.

Ah! Knowest thou the maiden all beauteous and fair,
Whom her merciless foes have left plundered and bare?
The force of my emblem too well cant thou feel,
For that suffering lorn one is our Grana Weal.

But the nobles shall bring back the true king again
And justice long slighted will come in his train;
The bullets shall fly — and the cannons shall peal —
And our Charles victorious espouse Grana Weal.

Irish Minstrelsy: James Hardinan, Vol. II, p.65

GRACE O'MALLEY

She left the close-air'd, land of trees
And proud MacWilliam's palace,
For clear, bare Clare's health-salted breeze,
Her oarsmen and her galleys
And where, beside the bending strand
The rock and billow wrestle,
Between the deep sea and the land
She built her Island Castle.

The Spanish captain, sailing by
For Newport, with amazement
Beheld the cannon'd longship lie
Moor'd to the lady's casement,
And, covering coin and cup of gold

In haste their hatches under,
They whisper'd "Tis a pirate's hold;
She sails the seas for plunder."

But no: t'was not for sordid spoil
Of barque or sea-board borough
She plough'd, with unfatiquing toil,
The fluent — rolling furrow;
Delighting, on the board back'd deep,
To feel the quivering galley
Strain up the opposing hill, and sweep
Down the withdrawing valley:

Or, sped before a driving blast,
By following seas uplifted,
Catch, from the huge heaps heaving past,
And from the spray they drifted
And from the winds that toss'd the crest
Of each wide-shouldering giant,
The smack of freedom and the zest
Of rapturous life defiant.

For, oh the mainland time was pent
In close constraint and striving,
So many aims together bent
On winning and on thriving;
There was no room for generous case,
No sympathy for candour; —
And so she left Burke's buzzing trees,
And all his stony splendour.

For Erin yet had fields to spare
Where Clew her cincture gathers
Isle — gemmed; and kindly clans were there,
The fosterers of her fathers:
Room there for careless feet to roam
Secure from minions' peeping,

For fearless mirth to find a home
And sympathetic weeping;

And generous ire and frank disdain
To speak the mind, nor ponder
How this in England, that in Spain,
Might suit to tell; as yonder,
Where daily on the slippery dais
By thwarting interests chequer'd
State gamesters played the social chess
Of politic Clanrickard.

Nor wanting quite the lovely isle
In civic life's adornings:
The Brehon's Court, might well beguile
A learned lady's mornings.
Quaint though the clamorous claim, and rude
The pleading that convey'd it,
Right conscience made the judgement good,
And loyal love obey'd it.

And music was sweeter far
For ears of native nurture,
Than virginals at Castlebar
To tinkling touch of courtier,
Where harpers good in hall struck up
The plantxty's gay, commotion,
Or, pipers scream'd from pennon'd poop
Their piobrach over ocean.

And sweet, to see, their ruddy bloom
Whom ocean's friendly distance
Preserved still unenslaved; for whom
No tasking of existence
Made this one rich and that one poor,
In golds illusive treasure,
But all, of easy life secure,
Were rich in wealth of leisure.

Rich in the Muse's pensive hour,
In genial hour for neighbour,
Rich in young mankind's happy power
To live with little labour;
The wise, free way of life, indeed,
That still, with charm adaptive,
Reclaims and tames the alien greed,
And takes the conqueror captive.

Nor only life's unclouded looks
To compensate its rudeness;
Amends there were in holy books,
In offices of goodness,
In cares above the transient scene
Of little gains and honours,
That well repaid the Island Queen
Her loss of urban manners.

Sweet, when crimson sunsets glow'd,
As earth and sky grow grander,
Adown the grass'd, unechoing road
Atlantic ward to wander,
Some Kinsman's humbler hearth to seek,
Some sick-bed side, it may be,
Or, onward reach, with footsteps meek,
The low, grey, lovely, abbey:

And, where storied stone beneath
The guise of plant and creature,
Had fused the harder lines of faith
In easy forms of nature;
Such forms, on tell the masters' pains
'Mong Roslins carven glories,
Or hint the faith of Pictish' Thanes
On standing stones of Forres;

The Branch; the weird cherubic Beasts;
The Hart by hounds o'ertaken;
Or, intimating mystic feasts,
The self-resorbent Dragon; —
Mute symbols, though with power endow'd
For finer dogmas' teaching,
Than clerk might tell to carnal crowd
In homily or preaching; —

Sit; and while heaven's refulgent show
Grew airier and more tender,
And oceans gleaming floor below
Reflected loftier splendour,
Suffused with light, of lingering faith
And ritual lights reflection,
Discourse of birth, and life, and death,
And of the resurrection.

But chiefly sweet from morn to eve,
From eve to clear-eyed morning,
The presence of the felt reprieve,
From strangers' note and scorning:
No prying, proud, intrusive foes
To pity and offend her: —
Such was the life the lady chose,
Such choosing, we commend her.

Sir Samuel Ferguson.

This song originated in County Leitrim around Ballinamuck and it is thought that it originated about 1798 with the survivors from Mayo of the Battle at Ballinamuck between the Franco-Irish forces and the English.

GRANUAILE

As the sunlight in its glory
Ever shines on fair Clew Bay
And Croagh Patrick old and hoary
Rises o'er the ruins grey
As the streamlets in the meadows
In their pride come dancing down
Nestled close among the mountains
Stands pleasant Newport Town.

Just a mile from where the turrets
Of the ancient town uprise
And the frowning peak of Nephin
Soars in grandeur to the skies
Lie a massive heap of ruins
In their loneliness sublime
Though scattered and dismantled now
By tyranny and time.

'Twas a proud and stately castle
In the years of long ago
When the dauntless Grace O'Malley
Ruled a queen in fair Mayo.
And from Bernham's lofty summit
To the waves of Galway Bay
And from Castlebar to Ballintra
Her unconquered flag held sway.

She had strongholds on her headlands
And brave galleys on the sea
And no warlike chief or viking
E'er had bolder heart than she.
She unfurled her country's banner
High o'er battlement and mast
And 'gainst all the might of England
Kept it flying 'til the last.

The armies of Elizabeth
Invaded her on land
Her warships followed on her track
And watched by many a stand
But she swept her foes before her
On the land and on the sea
And the flag of Grace O'Malley
Waved defiant, proud and free.

On the walls of Carrick Clooney
As the Summer sun went down
And its last bright rays were fading
On the spires of Newport town.
To the watchmen on the ramparts
There appeared in long array
A band of English spearmen
By the waters of Clew Bay.

To the walls flew Grace O'Malley
With her clansmen at her side
Who had often met the foemen
On the land and on the tide.
But she saw the marshalled strength
Of the English coming on
And the colour of their armour
That in polished brightness shone.

Soon before the frowning battlements
The English columns came
Whilst on the walls before them
Stood many a bristling gun.
Then forwards towards the barbacin
A herald quickly came
And demanded free admittance
In the English monarch's name.

He said 'My Royal Mistress
Sends her men-at-arms and me
With greetings good to all her friends
Who true and loyal be.
Her liegeman, Lord Hal Sydney
With all his spears awaits
For you to open wide to him
The Barbacin and gates!

'So tell your Royal mistress'
The dauntless Grace replied,
'That she and all her men-at-arms
Are scornfully defied.
She may own the fertile valley
Where the Foyle and Liffey flow
But tell her Grace O'Malley
Is unconquered in Mayo.'

'Our flag upon the battlements
Is to the breeze outhrown
And with God's grace we'll keep it there
In spite of Queen and throne.
There's many a brave O'Malley here
With me to man the walls
And rally round the flag we love
Until the last man falls!

'We want no English hirelings here
No soldiers of the Crown
We falter not before their spears
Nor cower beneath their frown.
No! clansmen, let your warcry ring
Defiance on the gale
And greet those braggart Saxons
With a shower of Irish hail.'

Then sprang upon the Britons
With many a loud hurrah
A band of fierce and rugged men
Well brazed in many a fray.
On every tower and battlement
The Irish kern appears
And fiercely flash their guns upon
The foe's advancing spears.

The dauntless Grace with Spartan soul
Stands on the outer wall.
Regardless of the shower of balls
That fast around them fall.
The English come with marshalled strength
And nerved with deadly hate
They fiercely clash through friends and foes
And gain the foremost gate.

But right before them face to face
The clansmen of Mayo
Start up and greet those robbers well
With thrust and sabre blow.
And rushing fierce as mountain stream
Through dark and flooded glen
Leaps to the gate, the dauntless Grace
And all her fearless men.

Hurrah! their spears are backward borne
Their blood red flag is down
And Sydney vanquished and pursued
Spurs hard to Newport Town.
This lesson taught the Saxon churl
To dread a Free-man's blow
When the dauntless Grace O'Malley
Ruled a Queen in fair Mayo.

The walls of Carrick Clooney
Now lie crumbling and low
Its battlements dismantled are
All moss o'er every stone.
But the rebel youth in Westport
Feel their Irish hearts aglow
When they tell how Grace O'Malley
Fought and conquered in Mayo.

There's many a fearless rebel
In Westport and Clew Bay
Who watch with longing eagerness
For Freedom's dawning day.
There's many a brawny mountaineer
Prepared to strike a blow
For the old Green Flag and Freedom
On the soil of brave Mayo.

Source: "Irish Minstrelsy" Vol. II

ORO AND WELCOME HOME

I

Welcome, O woman who was sorrowful
We were desolate while you were imprisoned.
Your lovely country in the hands of vandals
And you yourself — sold to the English.

Chorus:

    Oro — and welcome home,
    Oro — and welcome home,
    Oro — and welcome home,
    Would that the Summer is here.

II

Graine Mhaol is coming over the sea,
With a guard of young soldiers,
They are Irish, not English or Spannish
And they will rout the English.

III

Thanks be to God that I'm seeing
(Even if I only live for a week after!)
Grainne Mhaol and a thousand warriors
Announcing ruin on the English.

ORÓ, SÉ DO BHEATHA 'BHAILE

I

Sé do bheatha! a bhean ba leanmhar!
B'é ár gcreach tú bheith i ngéibhinn,
Do dhuiche bhrea i seilbh meirleach
'S tú diolta leis na Gallaibh.

Oró! sé do bheatha 'bhaile!
Oró! sé do bheatha 'bhaile!
Oró! sé do bheatha 'bhaile!
Anois ar theacht an tSamhraidh.

II

Tá Gráinne Mhaol ag teacht thar sáile,
Óglaigh armtha lei mar gharda;
Gaeil iad féin 's ni Gaill no Spainnigh,
'S cuirfid ruaig ar Ghallaibh.

III

A bhui le Rí na bhfeart go bhfeiceam,
Muna mbeam beo 'na dhiaidh ach seachtain,
Gráinne Mhaol agus mile gaiscioch
Ag fogairt fáin ar Ghallaibh.

Pádhraig Mac Piarais.

GRANUWEAL — An old Song

1.

A courtier call'd Dorset, from Parkgate did fail,
In his Majesty's yacht, for to court Granuweal;
With great entertainment the thought to prevail,
And rifle the charms of Granuweal.

Chorus:
> Sing Budderoo, Didderoo, Granuweal,
> The Fox in the Trap we have caught by the tail
> Sing success to the sons of brave Granuweal.

II

Says the courtier to Granu, if you will be true,
I will bring you to London, and do for you too;
Where you shall have pleasure that never will fail,
I'll laurel your Shamrock, sweet Granuweal.

III

Says Granu to Dorset, if that I would do,
Bring my fortune to London, my children would rue;
We would be like Highlanders eating of keal,
And cursing the union, says Granuweal.

IV

Says Granu, I always was true to my king;
When in war, I supply'd him with money and men.
Our love to King George with our blood we did seal,
At Dettingen battle, says Granuweal.

V

Says Granu, I always still lov'd to be free;
No foe shall invade me in my liberty.
While I've Limerick, Derry and the fort of Kinsale,
I'll love and not marry, says Granuweal.

VI

Says Granu, you see there's a large stone put in,
To the heart of the church, by the leave of the King.
The works of this stone shall be weigh'd in a scale,
With balance of justice, says Granuweal.

VII

I hope our brave Harington, likewise Kildare,
Our trade and our commerce once more will repair,
Our lives we will venture with greatest affail,
Against French and Spaniards, says Granuweal.

VIII

Now, my dear boys we've got shut of those bugs,
I' charge you my children, lie close in your rugs,
They'll hide like a snake, but will bite I'll be bail,
I'll give them shillelagh, says Granuweal.

POOR OLD GRANUAILE

My dream to some with joy will come and comes with grief to more,
As it did to me, my country, that dear old Erin's shore;
I dreamt I stood upon a hill beside a lovely vale,
And its there I spied a comely maid and her name was Granuaile.

Her lovely hair hung down so fair and she was dressed in green,
I thought she was the fairest soul that e'er my eyes had seen;
As I drew near I then could hear by the pleasant morning gale,
As she went along she sang her song saying "I'm poor old Granuaile".

In O'Connell's time in '29 we had no braver men,
They struggled hard both day and night to gain our rights again;
Still, by coercion we were bound and our sons were sent to jail,
"You need not fret, we'll Home Rule get" says poor old Granuaile.

I thought she had a splendid harp by her side she let it fall,
She played the tunes called Brian Boru, Garryowen, and Tara's Hall.
Then God Save Ireland was the next, and Our Martyrs who died in Jail,
"You need not fret, we'll have freedom yet" says poor old Granuaile.

When I wakened from my slumber and excited by my fight,
I thought it was the clear daylight, and I found that it was night;
I looked all round and could see naught but the walls of a lonely jail.
And that was the last I ever saw of poor old Granuaile.

Source: *Irish Street Ballads* collected and annotated by
Colm O Lochlainn, London 1928.

A NEW SONG CALLED GRANUAILE

All through the north as I walked forth to view the shamrock plain
I stood a while where nature smiled amid the rocks and streams
On a matron mild I fixed my eyes beneath a fertile vale
As she sang her song it was on the wrongs of poor old Granuaile

Her head was bare and her grey hair over her eyes hung down
Her waist and neck, her hands and feet, with iron chains were bound
Her pensive strain and plaintive wail mingled with the evening gale
And the song she sung with mournful tongue was Poor Old Granuaile.

The gown she wore was stained with gore all by a ruffian band
Her lips so sweet that monarchs kissed are now grown pale and wan
The tears of grief fell from her eyes each tear as large as hail
None could express the deep distress of poor old Granuaile.

On her harp she leaned and thus exclaimed My royal Brian is gone
Who in his day did drive away the tyrants every one
On Clontarf's plains against the Danes his faction did prepare
Brave Brian Boru cut their lines in two and freed old Granuaile.

But now, alas, I must confess, avengers I have none
There's no brave Lord to wave his sword in my defence — not one
My enemies just when they please with blows they do assail
The flesh they tore clean off the bones of poor old Granuaile.

Six hundred years the briny tears have flowed down from my eyes
I curse the day that Henry made of me proud Albion's prize
From that day down with chains I'm bound no wonder I look pale
The blood they drained from every vein of poor old Granuaile.

There was a lord came from the south he wore a laurel crown
Saying 'Grania dear, be of good cheer, no longer you'll be bound
I am the man they call great Dan, who never yet did fail
I have got the bill for to fulfil your wishes Granuaile."

With blood besmeared and bathed in tears her harp she sweetly strung
And oh the change, her mournful air from one last chord she wrung
Her voice so clear fell on my ear, at length my strength did fail
I went away and thus did say, "God help you, Granuaile".

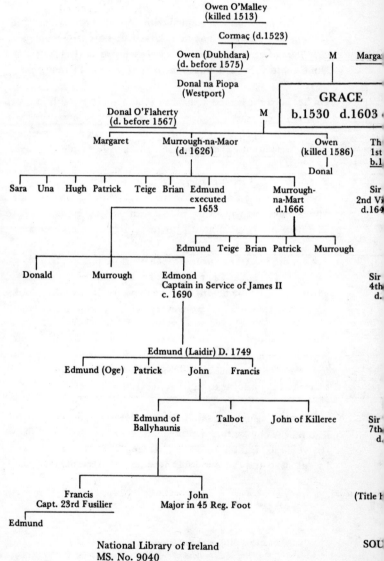

Owen O'Malley
(killed 1513)

Cormaç (d.1523)

Owen (Dubhdara)
(d. before 1575)

Donal na Piopa
(Westport)

M   Marga

GRACE
b.1530   d.1603

Donal O'Flaherty
(d. before 1567)   M

Margaret   Murrough-na-Maor   Owen   Th
              (d. 1626)   (killed 1586)   1st
                                                         b.1
                                        Donal

Sara Una Hugh Patrick Teige Brian Edmund   Murrough-   Sir
                                        executed   na-Mart   2nd Vi
                                        — 1653   d.1666   d.164

                                   Edmund Teige Brian Patrick Murrough

Donald   Murrough   Edmond   Sir
                              Captain in Service of James II   4th
                              c. 1690   d.

                    Edmund (Laidir) D. 1749

Edmund (Oge) Patrick   John   Francis

              Edmund of   Talbot   John of Killeree   Sir
              Ballyhaunis   7th
                                                                        d.

          Francis   John   (Title h
    Capt. 23rd Fusilier   Major in 45 Reg. Foot
Edmund

National Library of Ireland   SOU
MS. No. 9040
State Papers of Elizabeth I
Calendar of MS. of the Marquis of Salisbury (Vol IV)
"Linea Antiqua" Roger O'Ferrell

The Pedigree of
GRACE O'MALLEY
(b. 1530 – d. 1603 c.)

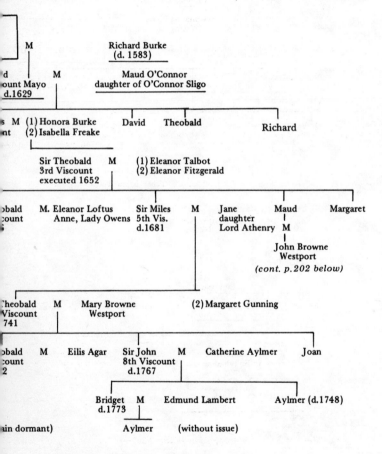

'Malley (Moher Sept)

M

Richard Burke
(d. 1583)

'd
ount Mayo   M
d.1629

Maud O'Connor
daughter of O'Connor Sligo

s M (1) Honora Burke   David   Theobald   Richard
nt   (2) Isabella Freake

Sir Theobald   M   (1) Eleanor Talbot
3rd Viscount   (2) Eleanor Fitzgerald
executed 1652

obald   M. Eleanor Loftus   Sir Miles   M   Jane   Maud   Margaret
count   Anne, Lady Owens   5th Vis.   daughter
5   d.1681   Lord Athenry M

                                                             John Browne
                                                             Westport
                                                             (cont. p.202 below)

Theobald   M   Mary Browne   (2) Margaret Gunning
Viscount   Westport
741

obald   M   Eilis Agar   Sir John   M   Catherine Aylmer   Joan
count   8th Viscount
2   d.1767

            Bridget   M   Edmund Lambert   Aylmer (d.1748)
            d.1773

ain dormant)   Aylmer   (without issue)

ES   "Iar-Connacht" Roderick O'Flaherty
            "History of the Commoners of Gt. Britain and Ireland" (Vol I)
            Burke.
            Public Record Office Dublin
            Chancery Bills

Decendants of Maud Bourke and John Browne

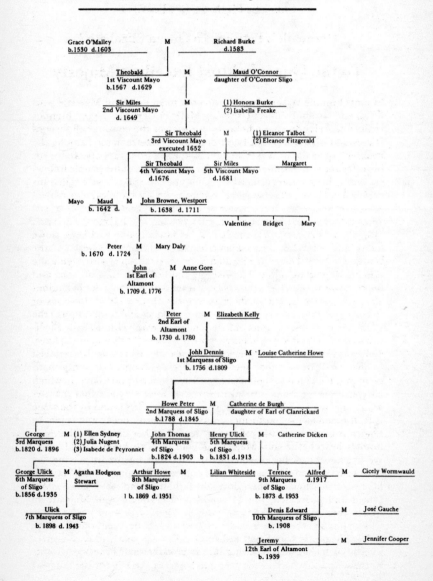

1988 EDITION SUPPLEMENT

Granuaile's Petition To Queen Elizabeth I

To the Queen's Most Excellent Majesty

In most humble Wise showeth unto your most excellent Majestie your loyall and faitefull subject Grany ny Mally of Conaght in your highnes realme of Ireland:- that wheras by meanes of the continnuall discord stirres and dissention that heretofore long tyme remained among the Irishrye especially in West Conaght by the sea side every cheeftaine for his safegard and maintenance and for the defence of his people followers and countrye took armes by strong hand to make head against his neyborhes which in like manner constrained your highnes fond subject to take armes and by force to maintaine her selfe and her people by sea and land the space of fortye yeares past. During which tyme she married Offlahertye being natural mother of his lawfull sone and heire nowe living and after his death married Mac William the cheefe of the Bourkes of West Conaght who died X yeares past, since which tyme she remaineth widowe and is likewise the mother of his lawfull sone and heyre nowe living. The countryes and teritories of which cheeftaines after the rude custome of their ancestores never yeilded doweries or thirds to the ladies thereof, and the rents services and reservation of the same was not certayne but confused the people for yelding to the cheeftaines whatever they would crave more than of ryght they aught to have. And now wheras by your gracious meanes the said province is reduced to that civill course that the cheeftaines freeholders or gents. hath compounded and is assigned what and how much he is to have; in which composition no order was taken for your fond subject what maintenance she aught to have of her former husbands lands and by the same is restrayned to use her former course to her utter decay and ruine: In tender consideracon wherof and in regard of her great age she most humbly besechethe your Majestie of your princely bounty and liberaltye to grant her some reasonable maintenance for the little tyme she hath to lyve. And wheras your said subjects two sones are the lawfull heyres of the lands of there foresaid fathers wherof they nowe stand seized and possessed, that it would please your Royall Majestie to direct your gracious letters to your L. Deputy of your said realme willing him to accept a surrender at her hands of her said sones yelding to Your Majestie your heyrs and successors such yearly rents as conveniently such lands may yeld and they to hold the same by letters patents to them and ther heyres for ever and to grant the like for the lands of

Walter Burgh Fitz Theobald Reogh and Shane Burke Mac William Mac
Moiler cosen germaine to her said son. And lastly that it would please
your Majestie to grant unto your said subject under your most gracious
hand of signet free libertye during her lyve to envade with sword and fire
all your highnes enemyes whersoever they ar or shal be without any
interruption of any person or persons whatsoever. Thus shall your said
subject according to her bounden duty ever remayne in all obedient
alleagance to the resist all remnants of rebellious enemies and pray
continually for your Majesties long life and prosperous reygne.

Source: State Papers Elizabeth I
             Public Record Office London.

Acknowledgement: Decyphered from the original by Anne Chambers for
"Granuaile The Life and Times of Grace O'Malley 1530-1603"
published by Wolfhound Press, Dublin.

Signed Letter by Theobald Bourke – Tibóid-na-Long (Toby of the
Ships), youngest son of Granuaile, to Anthony Brabazon, English
Commissioner of Connaught.

I have received your Honors letters and according as I have formerly
written that I should be advertised of the meeting doiet eight daies
before the appointeing thereof; I have not received the said advertise-
ment but the eight of this month wheras you would have me to meete
the IX of this month. Wherfore I desire yor. Honor to forbeare till the
eighteen of this month and in the meane time, wee will prepare our
complaints anhd agrievances and will be provided with provisions and
other necessaries wch cannot be done before that time. As for Odonelle
I perceive by his letters that he is likewise to answeare in that case for
others in Connought and do think that he will be ther doie before
menconed. Further for as much as Gallaway men do not furnishe us
with anie commodities wee desire yor. Honor to direct yor. warrant
unto the Mayor to th'end that we maye be furnished with such things as
ys expedient excepting munitions for warres and with all to send a
provision for those as will repaire for things to Gallawaye. Thus desir-
ing yor. Honor to do not faile therin. I bide yo hartely farwell. ffrom
camp the VIIIth of June 1596.

Signed Theobald Bourk

See above pages 136-139 and page 208 below for facsimile reproductions from the State Papers.

The Eighteen "Articles of Interrogatory"

TO BE ANSWERED BY GRANY NIMALY

1. Who was her father and mother
2. Who was her first husband
3. What sons she had by him. What be their names and where they live
4. What countries they have to maintain them withal
5. To whom they be married
6. What kin was O'Flaherty her first husband to Sir Mourrough M' Ne Dough O"Flaherty that is here now at the court
7. To answer the like question for her 2 husband and for his sons and their livings
8. If she were to be allowed her dower, or thirds of her husbands living of what value the same might be of
9. Where upon the Composition of Connaught there hath been any provision for the wives
10. Whether it be not against the Customs of Ireland for the wives to have more after the deaths of their husbands than they brought with them
11. How she hath had maintenance and living since her last husband's death
12. Of what kindred is Walter Bourgh fitz Tibalds and Shane Bourk mc Moyler to her son
13. What captains and countries lie next to her first husband's possessions
14. Who doth possess the house of Moriske upon the seaside in Owle O'Maly
15. What lands doth McGibbon possess in that country
16. Who doth possess the country named Carramore and Mayn Connell
17. Who doth possess the island of Achill and Kill castle
18. What kin was her last husband to Walter and Ulick Bourke

ANSWERS OF GRANY NY MALLY TO THE ARTICLES

To the first
Her father was called Doodarro O Mailly sometime chieftain of the country called Opper Owle O Mailly now called the barony of Murasky Murrisk her mother was called Margaret ny Mailly daughter to Conogher Omailly of the same country and family. The whole country of Owle O Mailly aforesaid have these islands viz. Inish Boffyny Cleria InishTwirke Inish arke Caher Inishdalluff Davellen and other small

islands of little value which and the rest of the mainland are divided into towns to the number of twenty and to every town four quarters or ploughs of land is assigned; out of every such quarter of land is yearly paid to her Majesty ten shillings called the composition rent. There is also in Connaught a country called Owle Eighter, otherwise the Lower or Nether Owle, containing fifty towns at four quarters the town, yearly paying the same rent, whereof the Sept of the Mailles in general hath twenty towns, the Bourkes of Mac William country other twenty towns and the Earl of Ormond ten towns.

To the second

Her first husband was called Donell Ichoggy Offlaherty and during his life chieftain of the Barony of Ballynehenssy, containing twenty-four towns at four quarters of land to every town paying yearly the composition rent aforsaid. After his death Teige Offlaherty the eldest son of Sir Morough now at court entered into Ballynehenssy afor said there there did build a strong castle and the same with the demain lands thereof kept many years. Which Teige in the last rebellion of his father was slain.

To the third

She had two sons by her said first husband the eldest called Owen Offlahertie married Katherin Bourke daughter of Edmond Bourke of Castle Barry by her he had a son named Donell Offlahertie, now living which Owen all his lifetime remained a true subject to Her Majesty under the government of Sir Nicholas Malby while he lived and under Sir Richard Bingham until July 1586 at which time the Bourkes of the McWilliams country and the sept of the Shoose [Joyce] began to rebel. The said Owen, according to Sir Richards special direction, did withdraw himself his followers and tenants, with all their goods and cattle into a strong island for their more and better assurance. Then having been sent against the said rebels five hundred soldiers under the leading of Captain John Bingham appointed by his brother Sir Richard Bingham as the lieutenant in those parts. When they missed both the rebels and their cattle they came to the mainland right against the said island calling for victualls; whereupon the said Owen came forth with a number of boats and ferried all the soldiers into the island where they were entertained with the best cheer they had. That night the said Owen was apprehended and tied with a rope with eighteen of his chief followers; in the morning the soldiers drew out of the island four thousand cows, five hundred stud mares and horses and a thousand sheep leaving the remainder of the poor men all naked within the island [they] came with the cattle and prisoners to Ballynehenssy afor said where John Bingham afor said stayed for their coming; that evening he caused the said eighteen persons without trial or good cause to be hanged among whom was hanged a gentleman of land and living called Thebault O Twohill being of the age of four score and ten years. The next night following a false alarm was raised in the camp in the dead of the night the said Owen being fast bound in the cabin of Captain Grene O Mulloy and at that instant the said Owen was cruelly murdered having twelve deadly wounds and in that miserable sort he ended his years and unfortunate days – Captain William Mostyn now at court and Captain Merriman and Captain Mordant were of that company. Her second son called Moroghe Offlahertie now living is married to Honora Bourke daughter to Richard Bourke of Derivillaghny in the Magheri Reagh within the county of Galway.

To the fourth

Moroghe her second son aforesaid and Donell son to her first son the aforesaid Owen murdered do possess and enjoy the fourth part of the Barony of Ballynehenssy aforesaid unto them descended from their ancestors which is all the maintenance they have.

To the fifth

This is answered more at large to the third article.

To the sixth

Her first husband by the mother's side of Sir Moroghe now at court was his cousins germain and also cousins both being descended of one stock and root of nine degrees of consanguinity asunder.

To the seventh

Her second husband was called Sir Richard Bourke Knight alias McWilliam chief of the Bourkes of Nether or Low Connought by him she had a son called Theobald Bourke now living he is married to Mewffe O'Connor sister to O'Connor Sligo now at court, his inheritance is about 40 quarters of land situated in the three baronies of Carry [Carra], Nether Owle and Galling [Gallen].

To the eighth

The countries of Connaught among the Irishry never yielded any thirds to any woman surviving the chieftain whose rent was uncertain for the most part extorted but now made certain by the composition and all Irish exactions merely abolished.

To the ninth

The Composition provided nothing to relieve the wife of any chieftain after his death wherin no mention is made of any such.

To the tenth

Among the Irishry the custom is that wives shall have but her first dowry without any increase or allowance for the same time out of mind it hath been so used and before any woman do deliver up her marriage portion to her husband she receives sureties for the restitution of the same in manner and form as she hath delivered it in regard that husbands through their great expenses especially chieftains at the time of their deaths have no goods to leave behind them but are commonly indebted; at other times they are divorced upon proof of precontracts; and the husband now and then without any lawful or due proceeding do put his wife from him and so bringeth in another; so as the wife is to have sureties for her dowery for fear of the worse.

To the eleventh

After the death of her last husband she gathered together all her own followers and with 1,000 head of cows and mares departed and became a dweller in Carrikahowlly in Borisowle parcel of the Earl of Ormond's lands in Connaught and in the year 1586 after the murdering of her son Owen the rebellion being then in Connaught Sir Richard Bingham granted her his letters of tuition against all men and willed her to remove from her late dwelling at Borosowle and to come and dwell under him, in her journey as she travelled was encountered by the five bands of soldiers under the leading of John Bingham and thereupon she was apprehended and tied in a rope, both she and her followers at that instant were spoiled of their said cattle and of all that ever they had besides the same and brought to Sir Richard who caused a new pair of gallows to be made for her last funeral where she thought to end her days, she was let at liberty upon the hostage and pledge of one Richard Bourke otherwise called the Devil's Hook when he did rebel fear compelled her to fly by sea into Ulster and there with O'Neill and O'Donnell staid three months; her galleys by a tempest being broken. She returned to Connaught and in Dublin received her Majesty's pardon by Sir John Perrot six years past and so made free. Ever since she dwelleth in Connaught a farmers life very poor bearing cess and paying Her Majesty's composition rent, utterly did she give over her former trade of maintenance by sea and land.

To the twelfth

Walter Bourke FitzThebalt and Shane Bourke FitzMeiller are cousins germain removed of one side viz. Walter son to Thebault, son to Meiller son to the said Walter Faddy. Thebault Bourke mentioned in the seventh article and born by Grany Ny Mailly son to Sir Richard Bourke her last husband, which Sir Richard was brother to the said Walter Faddy.

To the thirteenth
The country of her first husband is situated between Owle O'Mailley on the north west part, Mac William's country to the north east towards the country of Sligo, Sir Moroghe Offlaherties country on the east side towards Galway and the great bay of Galway on the south.

To the fourteenth
The castle town and lands of Morrisky is possessed by Owen M'Thomas O'Mailley now chieftain by the name of O'Mailley.

To the fifteenth
The Mac Gibbons have no lands by inheritance in any part of the country; farmers they are at will both to the Bourkes and to the O'Maillies.

To the sixteenth
She doth not know or understand Caremore or Moinconnell.

To the seventeenth
The island of Ackill is occupied by some of the Mailleys as tenants to the Earl of Ormond, as for Kill castle, she knoweth no town of that name.

To the eighteenth
Her last husband had two brothers Walter and Ulligge [Ulick] Bourke both died before she married Sir Richard Bourke, her said husband, their father was called David Bourke.

Source: Manuscript Facsimile of the Articles of Interrogatory "to be answered by Grany NiMaly".

A set of 18 questions drawn up by Lord Burghley, private secretary to Queen Elizabeth I, dated July 1593, with appropriate answers by Granuaile.

State Papers, Elizabeth I.
Public Record Office London.

Acknowledgement: Decyphered from the original by Anne Chambers for her book *Granuaile The Life and Times of Grace O'Malley 1530-1603* published by Wolfhound Press, Dublin.

NOTES

CHAPTER I

1. *A Chorographical Description of West Connaught*, p.140
2. *Ordnance Survey: Mayo. Vol. II*, p.97
3. *Annals of the Four Masters.* Vol. IV, p.815
4. *The Stranger in Ireland*, p.304
5. *A Chorographical Description of West Connaught*, p.333
6. *Ibid.*, p.332
7. *History of the Town and County of Galway*, p.83
8. *Ibid.*, p.64
9. *Ibid.*, p.201
10. *Anglo-Irish trade in the sixteenth century* in the Proceedings of the Royal Irish Academy. Vol. 36, p.317
11. *Ibid.*, p.317
12. *New History of Ireland*, p.36
13. *Annals of Ulster.* Vol. III, p.65
14. *Ibid.*, p.511
15. *S.P.I.* 63/158 No. 37
16. *The Irish Sword* Vol. I, p.158
17. *Calendar of State Papers*, Vol. CCVI, p.335
18. *Ibid.* Vol. CCVIII, p.436
19. *Ibid.*, p.418
20. *Annals of Ulster* Vol. II, p.33
21. *Ibid.*, Vol. III, p.511
22. *Ibid.*, p.65
23. The following account is based on *500 Years in the History of Murrisk Abbey*

CHAPTER II

1. *Fynes Morrison's Itinerary.* Vol. III, p.444
2. *Beginnings of Modern Ireland*, p.30
3. *The Course of Irish History*, p.178
4. *A Chorographical Description of West Connaught*, p.383
5. *Beginnings of Modern Ireland*, p.77

CHAPTER III

1. *Calendar of State Papers.* Vol. CLXX, p.132
2. *A Chorographical Description of West Connaught;* p.58
3. Chancery Bill No. R.63
4. *Social History of Ancient Ireland*, p.284
5. This and the following quotations are taken from *Irish Life in the Seventeenth Century.*

6. *Illustrations of Irish History, Discourse of Ireland*, p.357
7. *Irish Life in the Seventeenth Century*, p.338
8. *Ibid.*, p.29
9. *A Chorographical Description of West Connaught*, p.108
10. *Ibid.*, p.108
11. *Ibid.*, p.108
12. *Calendar of State Papers*, Vol. CCVII, p.5
13. *The Course of Irish History*, p.175
14. *History of the County Mayo*, p.171
15. *A Chorographical Description of West Connaught*, p.385
16. *Ireland Under the Tudors*, Vol. II, p.170
17. *History of the County Mayo*, p.178

CHAPTER IV

1. *Calendar of State Papers*, Vol. CLXX, p.132
2. *Ordnance Survey: Mayo. Vol. I*, p.1
3. *Irish Pedigrees*, Vol. II, p.675
4. *Gaelic and Gaelicised Ireland in the Middle Ages*, p.73
5. *Ordnance Survey: Mayo, Vol. I*, p.1
6. *Calendar of Carew Manuscripts.* Vol. II, p.49
7. *Ibid.*, p.49
8. *Ibid.*, p.353
9. *Ordnance Survey: Mayo. Vol. II*, p.99
10. *Ibid.*, p.88
11. S.P.I. 63/19 No. 56
12. S.P.I. 63/19 No. 186
13. *Calendar of Carew Manuscripts.* Vol. II, p.141
14. *History of the County Mayo*, p.188
15. *Ibid.*, p.188
16. *Ibid.*, p.188
17. *History of the County Mayo*, p.189
18. *Calendar of State Papers.* Vol. XCVI, p.406
19. *Calendar of State Papers.* Vol. XCIX, p.425
20. *Calendar of State Papers.* Vol. CLXX, p.132
21. *Ibid.*, p.132

CHAPTER V

1. *Annals of Loch Cé.* Vol. II, p.459
2. *Ireland under the Tudors.* Vol. III, p.122
3. *Ibid.*, p.125
4. *A Chorographical Description of West Connaught*, p.331
5. *Ibid.*, p.338
6. *Ibid.*, p.315

7. *Calendar of State Papers.* Vol. CLXX, p.132
8. *Ibid.,* p.132
9. *Ibid.,* p.132
10. *Salisbury Manuscripts,* Vol. IV, p.368
11. *Ibid.,* Vol. III, p.283
12. *Public Records in Ireland,* Report No. 16-20, p.69
13. *Ireland under the Tudors,* p.176
14. *History of the County Mayo,* p.228
15. *Ibid.,* p.230
16. *Calendar of State Papers* Vol. CLI, p.333
17. S.P.I. 3013 Nos. 62-66
18. S.P.I. 63/158 No. 37
19. *Calendar of State Papers,* Vol. CLXXI, p.141

CHAPTER VI

1. *Calendar of State Papers,* Vol. CLXVI, p.66
2. S.P.I. 63/170 No. 0204
3. *Calendar of State Papers,* Vol. CLXX, p.132
4. S.P.I. 63/170 No. 168, p.81
5. *English Court Life,* p.85
6. *Irish Pedigrees,* p.675
7. *Ibid.* Quoted in full above pp. 180-82.
8. S.P.I. 3013 No. 62-66
9. *Calendar of Salisbury Manuscripts,* Vol. IV, p.368
10. *Calendar of State Papers,* Vol. CLXXII, p.184
11. S.P.I. Calendar, Vol. CLXXIII, p.198
12. S.P.I. 63/179 No. 75
13. S.P.I. 63/179 No. 77
14. *Calendar of State Papers,* Vol. CLXXIX, p.315
15. *History of the County Mayo,* p.265

CHAPTER VII

1. *Scottish Mercenary Forces,* p.142
2. *History of the County Mayo,* p.265
3. *Calendar of Carew Manuscripts,* Vol. III, p.265
4. C.P.S.I. Vol. CC, p.376
5. *Elizabeth I and Her Parliaments,* p.142
6. *Calendar of State Papers,* Vol. CCVIII, p.436
7. *Ordnance Survey: Mayo.* Vol. II, p.11

BIBLIOGRAPHY

MAJOR SOURCES

1. *Annals of the Kingdom of Ireland by the Four Ulsters,* ed. and trans. John O'Donovan, (Dublin, 1851).

2. *Annals of Loch Cé,* ed. W. Hennessy, (London, 1871).

3. *Annals of Ulster,* ed. B. MacCarthy, (Dublin, 1893).

4. *Calendars of the Carew Manuscripts,* ed. J. S. Brewer and W. Bullen, (London, 1869).

5. *Calendars of the Cecil Manuscripts,* Historical Manuscripts Commission, (1883-1899).

6. *Calendars of the Manuscripts of the Marquis of Salisbury,* Historical Manuscripts Commission.

7. *Calendars of the State Papers of Ireland,* 1509-73; 1574-85; 1588-92; 1592-96; 1596-97; 1598-99; 1599-1600; 1600; 1601; 1601-03; 1603-06; 1606-08; 1608-10; 1625-32.

8. *Dictionary of National Biography,* ed. S. Lee. Vol. XIV.

9. *Galway Archaeological and Historical Society Journals.* Vols. I-VII, (Galway, 1903-1912).

10. Genealogical Office, Dublin Castle MSS. Nos. 699, 165, 155.

11. Irish Folklore Department, U.C.D. MSS Nos. 202, 86, 1134, 838.

12. *Irish Genealogist,* Vol. 1.

13. *Irish Sword,* Vol. 1.

14. *Leabhar na gCeart: The Book of Rights,* ed. and Trans. J. O'Donovan, (Dublin, 1847).

15. Linea Antiqua, Roger O'Ferrall (transcripts) MS. No. 482-5, Genealogical Office.

16. National Library of Ireland, Manuscripts Room. MSS. Nos. 9040, 4844, 8348.

17. Notes in the keeping of Mr. S. Gaisford St. Lawrence, Howth Castle.

18. *Ordnance Survey: Letters relating to the Antiquities of the County Mayo.* Vol. I, II. J. O'Donovan, (Dublin, 1862).

19. *Proceedings of the Royal Irish Academy,* Vol. 36.

20. Dublin Record Office, Dublin. Chancery Bills Nos. 1. 209, R.63, A.A. 150.

21. *Sidney State Papers,* 1565-70, ed. T. O'Laidhin, Irish Manuscripts Commission, (Dublin, 1962).

22. *State Papers of Ireland* (on microfilm), National Library of Ireland. Nos. 63/19.56, 186; 63/158.37; 63/170.168, 0204; 63/179.75, 77; 3013, 62-66.

23. *Ulster Journal of Archaeology,* Vol. IV (1856).

OTHER SOURCES

1. Bagwell, R. *Ireland under the Tudors,* Vols. I, II, III, (London, 1885-90).

2. Ball, F. *Howth and Its Owners,* (Dublin, 1917).

3. Burke, J. *History of the Commoners of Great Britain and Ireland,* Vol. I, (London, 1834).

4. Byrne, M. *Ireland Under Elizabeth,* (Dublin, 1903).

5. Callwell, J. *Old Irish Life,* (London, 1912).

6. Camden, W. *Britania,* (London 1695).

7. Canny, N. *The Elizabethan Conquest of Ireland: A Pattern Established 1565-76,* (Sussex, 1976).

8. Curtis, E. *A History of Ireland,* (London, 1937).

9. Derrick, J. *Image of Irelande,* (London, 1581).

10. Dunlop, R. *Ireland under the Commonwealth,* Vol. I, (Manchester, 1913).

11. Dutton, R. *English Court Life,* (London, 1963).

12. Falkiner, C. *Illustrations of Irish History and Topography,* (London, 1904).

13. Fallon, N. *The Armada in Ireland,* (London, 1978).

14. Graham, W. *The Spanish Armadas,* (London, 1972).

15. Hardiman, J. *History of the Town and County of Galway,* (Dublin, 1820).

16. Hardiman, J. *Irish Minstrelsy,* Vol. II, (London, 1831).

17. Holmes, G. *Ancient and Modern Ships,* (London, 1900).

18. Joyce, P. *Social History of Ancient Ireland,* Vol. II, (Dublin, 1913).

19. Knox, H. *The History of the County of Mayo,* (Dublin, 1908).

20. Leitch, M. *The Romance of Sails,* (London, 1975).

21. Mac Curtain, M. *Tudor and Stuart in Ireland,* (Dublin 1972).

22. Mac Lysaght, E. *Irish Life in the 17th Century,* (Cork, 1939).

23. McClintock, H. *Irish and Highland Dress,* (Dundalk, 1950).

24. McClintock, H. *Handbook of the Old Irish Dress,* (Dundalk, 1958).

25. Hayes-McCoy, G. *Scots Mercenary Forces in Ireland* (1939).
26. Mason, T. *The Islands of Ireland,* (London, 1936).

27. Maxwell, C. *The Stranger in Ireland,* (London, 1954).

28. Moody, T., Martin, F. (eds.) *The Course of Irish History,* (Cork, 1967).

29. Moody, T., Martin, F., Byrnes, F. (eds.), *A New History of Ireland,* Vol. III (Oxford, 1976).

30. Moryson, F. *An Itinerary* 3 pts. (London, 1617) New ed. in 4 vols. (Glasgow, 1907-8).

31. Neale, J. *Elizabeth I and her Parliaments 1584-1601*, (London, 1958).

32. Nicholls, K. *Gaelic and Gaelicised Ireland in the Middle Ages*, (Dublin, 1972).

33. O'Flaherty, R. *A Chorographical Description of West Connaught 1684*, (Dublin, 1846).

34. O'Hart, J. *Irish Pedigrees* Vol. I, 11, (New York, 1915).

35. O'Moráin, P. *Five Hundred Years in the History of Murrisk Abbey*, (Mayo News, 7 and 14 September, 1957).

36. Otway, C. *A Tour of Connaught*, (Dublin 1839).

37. Westropp, T. *Clare Island Survey*, (Dublin 1911).

38. Wilson, P. *The Beginnings of Modern Ireland*, (Dublin and London 1912).

INDEX

ERRATA

Page 60 line 13 should read: "become The MacWilliam Iochtarach . . ."

Page 78 line 8 should read: "Tibbot-ne-Long" (*ditto* pp 113 line 28, and 159 subheading)

Page 117 line 29 should read: "Sir William FitzWilliam"

Page 184 line 13 should read: "James Hardiman"

Page 206 line 2 should read: "by the Four Masters"